Praise for
Of Beauty and Substance A Backbone Guide for Women

"Beauty and Substance" is a rare gift for women seeking the courage to lead, to find the new backbone the leaders of the future require.
—Frances R. Hesselbein, President and CEO,
The Frances Hesselbein Leadership Institute

Susan Marshall's book is a must-read for anyone striving to live a life of significance. Becoming a woman of beauty and substance is a life-long journey, but Susan's insights, humor and guidance provide a wonderful roadmap to help you along the way.
—Suzanne Kelley, President, Waukesha County Business Alliance

Reading Susan Marshall's newest book "Of Beauty and Substance: A Backbone Guide for Women" is like sitting down to have a delightful conversation with the author. She encourages us to dream and yet delivers a direct, tell-it-to-you straight life road map. Amazing words to guide us!
—Peggy Stoop, Assistance Vice President, Private Banking

"Of Beauty and Substance : A Backbone Guide for Women" speaks to all women, young and old, at various stages of their lives. It clearly helps women understand that we share common areas that we need to assess since we are all forever becoming. Having a backbone enables the journey to be more purposeful and meaningful.
—Geneva Johnson, Retired President and CEO, Family Service America and Families International

A practical guide for women of all ages as they navigate the many roles they hold with an emphasis on how to maintain authenticity in the process.
—Janine Pesci, Firmwide Talent Development

"The only way to have a life that is interesting, meaningful and fun is to go create it." To me, that sums up Susan's lifelong work in one sentence. This is not solely a Backbone Guide for women to develop confidence, competence, and risk taking, it's a Guide for owning your rich and meaningful place in this world. Use it to go create the life that you want —don't wait for it to find you!
 —Heather N. Mangold, MBA, President, Mangold Creative, LLC

Contagious—inspirational, empowering, and enlightening. This Backbone Guide for Women illustrates that each of us have the propensity to take bigger steps, change, and grow. The education process doesn't end with books, school and structured classes.....it's the beginning to another type of learning in life through excellence. Susan is masterful at sharing her beacon light with others and enabling them to find their inner beauty and strength. Congratulations, Susan, for leading the way, and bringing all that read this book with you.
 —Marie O'Brien, President & CEO, Enterforce, Inc.

Susan Marshall has written a book that is bold, encouraging, and beautifully written. Her wisdom combined with her authentic vulnerability reaches into the corners of your heart and mind. Pick up this book and be inspired to embrace your own beautiful substance.
 —Kristin S. Kaufman, CEO and Founder of Alignment, Inc.
 and author of *Is This Seat Taken? Random Encounters that Change your Life*

Of Beauty and Substance

A Backbone Guide for Women

For Mary,
Good luck on
your new book!

Susan

Other books by Susan A. Marshall:

How to Grow a Backbone:
10 Strategies for Gaining Power and Influence at Work

Life: Be In It:
Words of Wisdom, Humor and Encouragement

Forthcoming books in the Backbone Guide Series:

Leveraging Your Genius: A Backbone Guide for Geeks

The Rise of Emerging Leaders:
A Backbone Guide for Young Professionals

Minding the Social Fabric:
A Backbone Guide for Non-Profit Leaders

Raising the Future:
A Backbone Guide for Parents

Empowering the Future:
A Backbone Guide for Educators

Of Beauty and Substance

A Backbone Guide for Women

Susan A. Marshall

MAVEN
MARK
BOOKS

MavenMark Books
Milwaukee, Wisconsin

Illustrations by Art Glazer
Cover design by Thomas Bruckbauer

Published by MavenMark Books,
An imprint of HenschelHAUS Publishing, Inc.
2625 S. Greeley St. Suite 201
Milwaukee, Wisconsin
www.henschelHAUSbooks.com

ISBN: 978-1-59598-313-8
E-ISBN: 978-1-59598-314-5
LCCN: 2014938952

Cataloging-in-Publication data block: PENDING

Printed in the United States of America.

For my daughters, Jennifer and Kelly,
And granddaughters
Peyton, Maya,
Lilly, Lexie, and Chloe:

*Though the world you navigate is different in so
many ways from the one I grew up in, your
beauty, strength, sense of purpose and sheer joy
at the adventure of life demonstrates the truth
that every woman blossoms in her own way in
her own time. You continue to inspire me as you
meet challenge with courage, disappointment
with grace, and 'those days' with serenity. Well,
most of the time.*
I love you all.

TABLE OF CONTENTS

Acknowledgments

I t is difficult to know where to begin acknowledging the many people who have touched and shaped my life as it pertains to the ideas in this book.

To Cathy and Art Lastofka, my Mom and Dad, for the very fact of life, I thank you. The lessons I learned by watching you over the years continue to have an impact on my thinking and actions, namely: waste nothing, work for what you want, save until you can afford it, and care for each other. Probably the biggest lesson you taught, however, is the power and magic of commitment. Through the toughest of times, your marriage promise to one another carried you through fear, anger, heart-break, and all manner of garden-variety frustration. I am proud of you both and honored to call you Mom and Dad.

Next, I must acknowledge the training and discipline instilled in me by Catholic nuns, who oversaw my grade school education. The two messages I heard over and over again: "You are a sinner," and "Do not hide your light under a bushel" created a mental puzzle worth solving.

When, as a young girl, I heard President John F. Kennedy admonish the nation to "ask what you can do for your country," I was thrilled by the notion that there was something I could do. This set me on a quest to discover, develop and contribute whatever capabilities I might have.

My paternal grandmother had a significant impact on my life despite the fact that she was relatively uneducated, never worked outside the home, and spent hours playing solitaire—with real playing cards—and drinking beer. Grandma had the gift of listening deeply and well, then turning my passionate questions back to me with a simple question. "What do you think?"

Of course, teachers, authors and even a celebrity or two shaped my ideas of femininity and authenticity, concepts that sometimes seemed aligned and sometimes devilishly disassociated.

Miss Stevens, my fifth-grade teacher mentioned in this book, modeled enthusiasm and joy. Mr. Jacobson, high school journalism teacher, taught me not only how to write effectively, but challenged me to think carefully before expressing my views.

Bani Mahadeva, professor of sociology at the University of Wisconsin-Oshkosh, praised my academic work and encouraged me to explore beyond prescribed boundaries. She inspired me to learn about other people and cultures to see and appreciate a magnificent world teaming with gifted "strangers."

Taylor Caldwell wrote long, insightful novels that laid bare the inner workings of the human mind and heart. As a 16-year-old having just finished reading *A Prologue to Love*, I wrote a passionate letter thanking her for shining a light on the dark places of the soul to celebrate the incredible depth of the human spirit. I never mailed it; I hadn't a clue how to find her. However, I read as many of her books as I could find and invited my daughters to find hardcover copies of her work any time they were at a loss for gift ideas at Christmas or birthdays.

Rosabeth Moss Kanter, Margaret Wheatley, Erma Bombeck, May Sarton, Betty Friedan, and Maya Angelou—each so different and all so talented, fed my hungry mind with their unique insights and personalities.

Mary Tyler Moore portrayed a single, local news producer in Minneapolis in one of my favorite TV shows, *The Mary Tyler Moore Show*. She was smart and funny and naïve and good and I wanted to be just like her. Katherine Hepburn portrayed a different sort of woman—tough, pragmatic, fearless and passionate and I wanted to be just like her, too. Another puzzle to solve.

I am grateful to a wide variety of co-workers and colleagues, with whom I have shared the struggle to adapt to tumultuous change. Some adapted, some did not. Of those who did adapt, some merely survived, while others thrived. All were instructive.

Additionally, to students of my MBA Leadership class and participants in Confidence Clinics, Backbone Boot Camps, and various workshops, your engagement in bold or quiet ways challenges my thinking and makes me better. I thank you.

My daughters, Jennifer and Kelly, have been instrumental in examining the timeliness of my ideas and the timelessness of my values. The world turns in wild and unpredictable ways, pulling us hither and yon. Knowing and maintaining your center of faith provides a blessed equilibrium while helping others find their way, too. Having these two beautiful women in my corner has been one of the greatest gifts of my life.

Speaking of gifts, the church ladies: Lois Winn, Marlene Schumacher, Joanne Zaferos, Betty Reul, and Mary Thiele are my ongoing beacons of support and chastisement. Our monthly summit meetings over coffee and gluten-free goodies refresh, refine, and occasionally reframe my thinking, sometimes in surprising ways. They are dear to me.

Kira Henschel, my wise and patient publisher, has observed my on-again/off-again efforts on this book, pushing me to proceed while graciously ignoring the passage of seemingly unproductive time. Of course, she understands the difficulty of corralling thoughts and working to express them with relevance and cogency and I admire and appreciate her kind counsel. With five more Backbone Guides in our collaborative future, I am prodded to pick up the pace!

I am similarly grateful to illustrator Art Glazer, who created the delightful illustrations for the original book, *How to Grow a Backbone: 10 Strategies for Gaining Power and Influence at Work.* Art's work has been featured in *Reader's Digest*, the *New York Times, Consumer Reports, Prevention Magazine, Sky Magazine-Delta*, the *Burlington Free Press*, the *Hartford Courant, Financial Times*, Avon books, Harper Collins, and a variety of corporate newsletters and annual reports, including Marriott, Sprint, Lucent, Ciba, Ernst & Young, IBM, Veterinary Forum, and Philip Morris. You may have also seen his work at New York City Transit. Art's skill in depicting emotion through iconic characters is delightful and deeply inspiring. I am honored that he has agreed to illustrate the entire Backbone Guide Series.

Tom Bruckbauer, talented graphic artist and friend for more than 20 years, created the iconic logo for Backbone Institute and designed the cover for this book. Tom has also agreed to be part of the Backbone Guide Series creative team, responsible for designing each of the covers. Check out backboneinstitute.com/ backbone-guide-series for a sneak preview. Tom's eye for precision and knowledge of production is a tremendous asset to this work. Thanks, Toemaas!

There are hundreds more people who have influenced me in the past and continue to touch my heart and mind today. It is impossible to name them all. I pray that every human with whom I have engaged will be as refreshed in some way from our encounter as I have been by you. Whether you realize it or not, you are making memories. I thank you all.

—Susan A. Marshall

INTRODUCTION

Fourteen years ago, I wrote a book called *How to Grow a Backbone: 10 Strategies for Gaining Power and Influence at Work*. Initial reaction was guarded. No one would personally admit to needing the advice the book offered, but almost everyone knew someone who did: a child, co-worker, spouse, partner, colleague, even a parent, teacher, or boss.

Since its publication, I have had the privilege of working with thousands of people one on one and in groups; via telephone and electronic media; informally, and at conferences and workshops. The learning for all has been fantastic.

Two questions have come up over and over again. The first, "Did you write that book primarily for women?" No. In fact, more male than female behaviors prompted me to write the book.

The second question, "How are we doing today compared to then?" Meaning: Are we stronger, more confident, and more inclined to take intelligent purposeful risk than we were more than a decade ago? No, we are not stronger or more confident and our propensity for taking intelligent, purposeful risk has declined precipitously. So much so that the *Wall Street Journal* featured a front-page story on June 3, 2013 headlined, "Risk Aversion Infects US Workers, Entrepreneurs."

Theories abound as to why this is. Depending on who you listen to, it's because of failing schools, inept or corrupt government, spoiled kids, rotten parents, a struggling economy, rejection of religion, wimpy efforts at promoting diversity, and an overall loss of faith in just about everything. Finger pointing is popular, but it solves nothing.

Additionally, the scale for measuring competence has become indulgent and indistinct, as though one level of achievement is as good as another. Standards have fallen over the past decade as we have relaxed expectations with the mistaken notion that by lowering standards, more people would achieve them—gain competence—and thus build confidence or, rather, self-esteem. In relaxing expectations, we have made reaching them less exciting and achieving them less noteworthy.

Backbone is a combination of three essential elements:

1) Competence, being good at things;
2) Confidence, having a positive expectation for a favorable outcome (thanks to Rosabeth Moss Kanter for this definition as written in her 2004 book *Confidence*); and
3) Risk taking, the act of moving past your comfort zone to do something unfamiliar.

Working in concert, these elements form an effective, everyday learning system that supports growth and leads to life-changing effort. People with strong backbones are wonderful to live, work, and play with.

Each of us can use these elements to make our lives different in the future than they have been in the past. And I mean just that—different. Any time we change what we are accustomed to doing, life gets different; sometimes better, but not always. That there is no guarantee in this regard is what keeps many people stuck in situations and mindsets that do not work particularly well. The fear of making things worse is a powerful antidote to taking purposeful risk.

This fear can be overcome. It is possible to develop competence through challenge, find confidence in mastery, and learn through doing that risk taking is a worthwhile developmental endeavor, even when results don't immediately match expectations. The struggle is meaningful.

The writing of this book has spanned several years and has challenged me in significant ways. It has changed tone each time I have come back to it. Three years ago, when I first started putting thoughts to paper, I was angry. Angry at a culture that was sick. Angry that leaders were few and far between. Angry that in the United States of America, corruption and deceit were commonplace and therefore of little note. Angry that women were being distracted by the harpy voices of advertisers promising eternal youth and material wealth, while chasing fame through notoriety. In the process, women were becoming hollow, shallow, and sick.

I did not want to produce a book that was darkly cynical or cynically resigned to darkness. So I waited. In the meantime, I continued working with various clients on leadership development, speaking on *Backbone*, and developing workshops to promote confidence and intentional behavior. I noted struggles and successes, hopes and fears, mistakes and renewed determination and outcomes that range from predictable to transformational.

While we all face the universal challenge of stepping outside our comfort zones to learn and grow, there are differences in the obstacles we face. At this writing, in addition to this *Backbone Guide for Women*, I envision books for young professionals, geeks, non-profit leaders, parents and educators. You can learn more and join in a conversation at www.backboneinstitute.com. Check out upcoming books in the series and let me know which one you would like to see next. I would love to hear your thoughts.

I'd also welcome your reaction to the thoughts and ideas in this book. Over the years, I have formed opinions about what works and what doesn't, recognizing that context often defines success. My experience, though deep, is unique and limited. I value other perspectives and the chance to learn from them.

That said, I know that good intentions never justify bad behavior. I know that the skills and confidence you develop over the course of your lifetime will either allow you to be welcomed into any setting you wish to visit or keep you out of some places you yearn to go. I also know that the success and happiness you enjoy in your life is a product of the decisions you make—and the stories you tell yourself—along the way.

Nothing is permanent until life ends. Everything can be changed and many things can be fixed. No mistake disqualifies you forever if you are willing to learn. Similarly, no success lasts forever. Those who understand that the journey is more important than the destination are wise, indeed. They tend to be luckier and more resilient than others, too.

What creates a woman of beauty and substance? Hardship. Loss. Disappointment. Mistakes. Poor decisions. Forgiveness. Acceptance. Love. The tough stuff we label as bad and try to avoid and the good stuff we wish we could learn and apply more quickly. Through struggle, we learn lessons about our true strength. By facing hardship, we recognize that life is difficult and that we are up to the challenge of living it well. In forgiveness, we find relief and peace. When we forgive others, we discover our capability to survive hurtful words and deeds. In this strength, we move forward.

This book is about you and your remarkable future. In it, we will explore specific challenges and provide suggestions, perhaps a different perspective, and certainly encouragement to take yourself in hand to start creating a stronger, happier, more fulfilling life. It doesn't matter where you are now. It doesn't matter what anyone else is doing. All that matters is what you are willing to learn and do.

The truth is that you have within you everything you need to be a beautiful, important woman of substance. While the world encourages you to carefully maintain the outward packaging you carry with you, the good stuff is inside. Let's turn our attention and energy toward discovering, developing, celebrating, and sharing that inner person, shall we? That is the mission of this book. I hope you will be inspired to advance your personal voyage of discovery. There is only one you.

And here's a big truth: ***The rest of us need you***.

CHAPTER ONE

BEAUTY, SUBSTANCE, AND BACKBONE

Beauty: By Whose Standards?

"Beauty is in the eye of the beholder," wrote Plato, a Greek philosopher in the 3rd century BC. While this may be true for art and architecture, it is patently untrue for women. What I see in a painting by Picasso or a building in St. Petersburg, Russia, may be entirely different and thus valued differently than what you see, but a woman's value is undeniable. Her beauty—her self—is not dependent upon the approval or rejection of those who might gaze upon her.

Ah, but don't we often believe the opposite? Don't we believe that unless those around us look at us with kind and approving eyes, we are somehow deficient?

Truth is, many women—maybe you—believe that if her features or physical stature do not match those of glamour models, fitness gurus, or TV and movie stars, she has some work to do. And it's no wonder, for this is the relentless message we receive from beauty products marketers everywhere. You cannot turn on a TV, go online or pick up a magazine without some gorgeous image inviting you to look just like her.

The images we call beautiful today are created by fashionistas: art directors, graphic designers, and other creatives, enhanced by a stunning suite of technologies, and presented to the world as standards for all to seek. The air brushing of models has become a classic example of how women are sold unreality; then encouraged to achieve it in real life.

In the United Kingdom, the subject of airbrushing gained strong attention in 2011, when a *LiveScience* survey revealed the extent of young women's desire to look like magazine models.

> *Everything has beauty, but not everyone sees it.*
> ~ Confucius

One-third of female college students said they would trade at least one year of their life to have their ideal body. Two percent said they would sacrifice ten years for a better body. Ninety-three percent had negative thoughts about their looks within the past week and although 78 percent of the women surveyed were normal weight—or even underweight—79 percent of the survey group said they wanted to lose weight. I joke about this when I'm speaking to women by saying that every woman on the planet at some point in her life has had the exact same goal: to lose weight. Which of course is not a goal but an unspecific wish.

Another UK website asked in August 2011: *Is airbrushing in magazines and advertisements out of control?* Ninety-four percent of respondents said yes. Just six percent said no.

Now this may seem like no-brainer stuff. But the impact it has on women's confidence is nothing to brush off (pun intended). The more time you spend studying fashion or fitness magazines, imagining an ideal you that only faintly resembles the real you, the more likely you are to experience frustration, sadness, or depression. Why would you do that to yourself?

It is true that we often try on different styles before finding our own. It's great fun! And harmless, so far as it goes. However, a growing number of women are reluctant to mature beyond this stage. With the help of plastic surgeons, personal trainers, youth-preserving products and treatments, and relentless advertising, some women try to hold onto the dew of youth despite the passage of time—sometimes a lot of time. What emerges over the years is a plastic shell housing a remarkably undeveloped and frighteningly fragile human being.

It had been several years since I last saw Carelle. Truth is, we had never been close friends, but when we worked together, we enjoyed an amicable relationship. She is a gifted artist and always looked the part. Stylishly dressed and impeccably groomed, she carried herself like a movie star. One afternoon before leaving work, I stopped in the ladies room. There she was with full make-up bag touching up her face. I kiddingly asked if she had a hot date waiting, and she looked at me with what seemed a strange expression. She didn't respond and I didn't say anything more. Later that week I overheard a bit of gossip. Carelle was planning to have a face lift.

As too many of these stories go, I hardly recognized her when I saw her. It was obvious that she had undergone more than one procedure—I couldn't begin to guess how many or for what desired outcome. What struck me was the flatness of her eyes. When she smiled, her expression was oddly joyless, a grimace. Her voice, too, had an eerie quality to it, almost hollow. I couldn't help but think how fragile she looked.

This fragility destroys true happiness and makes our society increasingly unstable. The strength and depth that is required not only to survive but thrive is literally being starved out of existence as we spend increasing amounts of time and energy trying to preserve our packaging.

Now, I am not saying that the antidote is to turn away from physical beauty. Heavens no! If you are blessed with a gorgeous face and enviable figure, by all means care for and enjoy them! But please don't make them the center of your life or the source of your happiness.

As fate would have it, a royal wedding took place while I was working on this book, providing yet another perspective on beauty. Prince William married his long-time love, Kate Middleton, now referred to as Catherine, the Duchess of Cambridge.

Catherine was stunningly beautiful on her wedding day. Nearly every woman I talked to sighed over the wonderfulness of the day. How gorgeous Catherine was, how lucky to be marrying into royalty, and how happy she seemed. Of course there were detractors, there always are. One woman thought she looked "horsey." A few others snidely remarked on how different Kate's life would be under the thumb of royal expectations.

As I watched video of Catherine on her wedding day, I was looking through the lens of beauty and substance. Catherine is a woman of great physical attractiveness: slim, fair of complexion, luxurious long dark hair, beautiful white teeth, clear eyes, a graceful carriage. She is also a woman of financial means, though in the context of British society, she is a commoner. Her family created great wealth as entrepreneurs, a livelihood that had not theretofore been acknowledged as noteworthy or a cause of pride, especially when compared to the Royal Family.

So here was a woman of common background marrying into the Royal Family. The Royal Family! Kate Middleton married the eldest son of the deceased beloved Princess Diana. You can hear the disapproving whispers and see the raised eyebrows, can't you?

Did she look cowed? No. Did she appear insecure about her worthiness? Not for one second. Quite the contrary, she looked absolutely joyful. Confident, poised, pleased and proud to be taking this step into the future with her long-time love.

> *Never lose an opportunity for seeing anything beautiful, for beauty is God's handwriting.*
> —Ralph Waldo Emerson

Despite his family background!

Kate's outside packaging is spectacular. Her inner serenity and peaceful joy make her radiant.

And so it is with you. The woman inside your wrapping is incredibly beautiful in ways that are not always visible on the surface. The woman inside is stronger than any test of physical might could measure. She has all the ingredients necessary for creating the wonderful life you want.

True beauty evokes a smile in the mind and heart, as well as on the face. Think about that for a moment. Beauty makes us feel good. It can be found in the glorious colors of a sunset, heard in the morning call of a songbird, felt in the gentle touch of a loved one.

Beauty creates connection. It evokes feelings of goodness and joy, power, serenity and love. Do you realize that every time you reach out to connect with others you are demonstrating beauty?

Conversely, the more time you spend gazing in the mirror, especially after studying glossy photos of beautiful models, the more likely you are to feel discontent worm its way into your mind and heart. The happiest and most productive women are out in the world warts, wrinkles and all! The beauty of their actions creates goodness wherever they go.

Here is a timeless reminder from the online *Meditations For Women* by Jane Powell:

> *You don't need a perfect figure, a huge and expensive wardrobe or a brilliant hairdresser, to make you a beautiful woman. Beauty is waiting there inside your soul, ready to be brought out. Your joy in life and passionate pursuits make you sparkle and radiate excitement and energy. Your sexy confidence and enthusiasm light up your face and bring a swing to your walk. Your serenity, generosity and sensitivity are mirrored in your eyes and in your beautiful smile. You are a beautiful woman—know it, believe it and live it!"*
>
> © Meditations for Women / www.MeditationsForWomen.com

And one from Elizabeth Kubler-Ross, a Swiss American psychiatrist, pioneer in near-death studies and author of the groundbreaking book *On Death and Dying*. She wrote, "People are like stained-glass windows. They sparkle and shine when the sun is out, but when darkness sets in, their true beauty is revealed only if there is a light from within."

Substance: On What Terms?

Substance is a quality you may admire and strive for without being sure of what it is or how to get it. It's a tough term to define, though when something is substantial it is strong, firm, stout. It is the light from within that Kubler-Ross refers to, a life-enriching mix of fortitude, courage, strength, patience, intelligence, and persistence. It is a person's character and the essence of the irrepressible human spirit. As my grandpa used to say, "I wanna know what you're made of."

While beauty is built in, substance is a by-product of living. You cannot read about it, listen to MP3s, or watch DVD demonstrations in order to develop substance. You cannot put on certain clothes, hang out in certain places or imitate a favorite role model and expect to build substance. You gain it by trying things, making mistakes, learning to overcome disappointment, and figuring out how to take your place in a crowded and competitive world.

Misfortune had made Lily supple instead of hardening her, and a pliable substance is less easy to break than a stiff one.
—Edith Wharton

Substance is formed on life's terms, which means that events beyond your control will sometimes require you to respond whether you are ready or not. This can be an exciting proposition if you are engaged in growth and learning. Discovering hidden strengths and uncovering latent capabilities can be enormously uplifting. On the other hand, building substance under pressure can be a terrifying experience if you have no idea about your true capacity and have not yet learned how to cope.

It used to be that a girl had to try out in order to win the privilege of doing things she wanted to do. Cheerleading, pompoms, student government, debate, sports. There were even writing contests to win such things as birch trees. I won one of those in fourth grade. The birch tree that was planted in my front yard then was the same one I sat under as a high school dreamer, plucking away on my mother's used steel-stringed guitar, imagining myself as Joan Baez. It is slightly embarrassing to remember this now. But those dreams and the effort expended in the pursuit of them created a core. However uncertain its strength in the beginning, this developing core formed beliefs about identity, desire, aspiration, conviction, and determination.

I wanted to be a rock star back then. I spent hours in my room singing to popular songs with my hand cupped to my ear, trying to hear how I really sounded. Not trusting this, I also sang into a tape recorder. Good thing. I was awful. That particular dream died at an early age.

This is an important point! When you had to earn a place, you either had what it took to do the thing you wanted to do or you didn't. If you didn't make the cut for the debate team or cheerleading or student government or whatever you aspired to, you grieved and then got on with life. No supporter back then had the time to whisper continual encouragement in the face of dismal performances. You licked your wounds and turned your attention elsewhere. You learned by doing.

I was a junior in high school when the Junior Miss Pageant came to town. It was a feeder event to bigger and better pageants including Miss Wisconsin, where I lived, and of course Miss America. I don't recall ever having seen it in high schools where I lived; in fact most beauty pageant candidates came from county fairs.

Not wanting to miss something so exciting, I entered the Junior Miss pageant even though I was certainly no beauty (acne owned me) and had yet to discover any particular talent. One of my happiest friends and unwitting mentors was a lithe and athletic gymnast; I secretly yearned to be just like her. So I decided to imitate her for the talent portion of the contest.

Let me pause a moment to describe our differences. Pam was 5 feet 9 inches tall and lean. Her muscles looked like rubber bands. I was 5 feet 3 inches tall and chunky. My muscles looked like building blocks. She was a dancer. I was a linebacker.

No matter. I picked a Carol King song that I loved and choreographed a routine that I practiced in my back yard for hours. Mind you, I knew nothing of choreography—the use of space and movement—but I had a passion for the song. *"Let the earth move under your feet"* seemed a fitting inspiration for my work.

I saw Mom look out the kitchen window an evening or two as I practiced in the dark with the porch light on. Though I'm sure she was careful to mask her expression, I perceived pity. Maybe she shook her head ever so slightly. But I soldiered on. I was determined to make an impression at this pageant!

Turns out I did. Almost fell off the stage. My underwear poked out from underneath my body leotard. I looked as goofy as I felt. The girl who won the pageant played to her strength, which was writing. She read an essay. I couldn't image a more uninspiring display of talent! Being a pretty good writer myself, I thought it too mundane for a pageant, which is why I tried to dance. Lesson learned. Substance initiated.

The question I would like you to consider is this: "What if you were born perfect?" What if you arrived at precisely the right time with exactly the right gifts of temperament and skill and capacity in order to live the life that only you can live, leaving behind a legacy that only you can create?

Every woman on Planet Earth wrestles with some big questions. They are big because they defy quick or certain answers. More befuddling, they may elicit different answers at different times. These big questions are powerful! They can stimulate your curiosity and fuel change. But only if you approach them in the right frame of mind. I suppose there are many big questions, but these four are especially important. If you take time to consider them carefully, you will find keys to living the kind of life every woman wants. A life of purpose and meaning. A life that matters. A life of beauty and substance.

1) Who are you?

2) What set of unique talents/gifts were you given at birth?

3) What might you make of these gifts to create a rich and satisfying life for yourself and those you love?

4) What contribution would you like to make?

The first question, "Who are you?" is a tough one. What does it really ask? Who are you in what context? You are a female of a certain age living in a certain location doing certain things in pursuit of a certain something. Not very satisfying as an answer, is it? I think when you try to answer this big question by answering smaller questions about preferences or talents or a job title, you get a catalog of personal traits or characteristics that doesn't measure up to the real person you are.

How, then, to describe the fullness of you? Let's see what happens as you answer the next couple of questions.

"What unique talents/gifts were you given at birth?" You have many! Your physical makeup and features mark you as one of a kind. Your body size and shape, hair color, eye color, blood type, physiology (how your body works without your knowing!), and many other characteristics of your organism are unlike those of any other human on earth. That's quite remarkable. And worth exploring, understanding and celebrating! No one else is like you. Never can be.

The flip side of that coin, of course, is that you are not like anyone else, either. You can't have Rachel's eyes or Mandy's hair or Debbie's long legs. If you think about it, these features would probably look silly on you. They wouldn't fit the rest of your package.

I remember many years ago spending an afternoon at a lake with a group of people I did not know well. An acquaintance from high school had invited me with the idea that it would be good for me to broaden my circle of friends. Naturally, I brought teenage uncertainty to the outing. Who were these people? How did they behave? What would be expected of me? The hellos were awkward, but soon I noticed a woman who seemed quite popular. She was sitting near the water in a two-piece bathing suit. Her skin was deeply tanned, her blond hair bleached nearly white by the sun. She had a contagious laugh and a genuine smile as she spoke with others. She was fat.

Now I don't think I am exposing any secret when I say that high school girls can be brutal to one another, particularly when it comes to physical appearance. This woman was a bit older, probably in her mid- to late-twenties. If she noticed the snickers because of her size, she was completely unfazed by them. Her happy self-acceptance was remarkable to see. All these years later, I still remember how reassured I felt and how much I hoped one day to be as comfortable in my skin, whatever its size, as that lady was in hers. Although she was completely unaware of it, she inspired me. You can do the same.

The next most obvious set of gifts you have involves that amazing engine you carry around inside your head—your brain. How you process information, the conclusions you draw, the experiences that shape your thinking, all these and many other brain related functions are also unique to you. Where you were born determines your first set of life rules and many of your earliest memories. Culture is the term we give to this phenomenon, this way of living. Your family of origin sets that cultural base and shapes your early life. If you grew up without this family influence, your experiences will provide a very different frame of reference than someone who grew up within a family structure.

In the same way, you have unique preferences—likes and dislikes—that belong only to you. While you and your friends may love pizza, the way you like your crust, sauce, toppings and spices will be different from theirs. I never got the idea of putting pineapple on pizza, but I know a bunch of people who love it. To each her own, as they say.

And so on with everything else about you that is unlike any other person on the planet. You are a special one-of-a-kind creature!

Understanding this uniqueness is a critical part of appreciating and celebrating who you are. Just as with physical attributes, no one experiences life quite the way you do, nor you like anyone else. Wishing you had someone else's life is as futile as wishing you had someone else's body parts. It wouldn't suit you! Your life defines a pathway that is brand new to the world. No one else can own it. No one can understand it, either, unless you share it.

Which brings us to the third big question. How can you develop your unique gifts to create a rich and satisfying life for yourself and your loved ones? This is a loaded question, so let's unpack it a bit.

First, let's look at the assumptions. By posing this question, I assume you know and appreciate that you have gifts and that they are unique to you. But maybe no one ever told you this. Maybe you, like many women, have spent a great deal of time feeling sad because you were not blessed with physical beauty or notable intellect or famous parents. This feeling of sadness is pervasive in our culture and it makes me sad because it is such a waste of time, energy and happiness. Enough with the sadness! Start noticing your gifts. Make a list of them. Never mind how they compare to someone else's, they are yours to develop and use. All yours, given to you free at birth. That's something to get excited about!

My second assumption is that you are indeed interested in making something of your gifts. Again, this may be a strange idea if no one has encouraged you to grow. As you begin to discover your talents, you may naturally begin to wonder what you can do with them. There is risk here! This act of wondering may make people close to you uncomfortable. As a non-traditional adult college student in my thirties, I began to notice how some of the women in my classes changed. Some of them found their voices for the first time. Some became visibly more confident as they learned to express their ideas in writing and in presentations. A few started complaining about their stultifying marriages or husbands who tried to make them feel guilty about working to advance themselves.

When I found myself among a growing number of divorced women for reasons that included this discomfort with uneven growth, I learned in a very painful way that life is risky when you vow to grow. This sort of risk is not something you embrace with glee and in fact the fear of upsetting the status quo keeps many women stuck in places they don't want to be. We'll talk more about this later.

My third assumption is that you want a life that is rich and satisfying (according to your definition, not mine). Who doesn't? But if you don't know it is possible, you don't have reason to think seriously about it. You may have reached an age or stage of your life in which you think your best years have passed and no amount of wishing or dreaming or working or scheming is going to bring you any more happiness than you have already enjoyed. This is a common feeling and it causes that sadness I mentioned earlier. It, too, is a false notion. It's a bad story you're telling yourself.

As an elder myself, I can tell you with certainty that in time everything old is new again. Diagramming sentences. Learning grammar. Practicing manners. Dealing with disappointment. I'll challenge you throughout this book to find a better story for yourself—indeed, to create a life story that fits you now, that celebrates your gifts, and that motivates you to truly appreciate where you are and where you'd like to go next. This is not just pie -in-the-sky thinking and it is not something that comes quickly or easily. Anyone who tries to tell you otherwise is lying to you.

My final assumption in the question, "How can you develop your unique gifts to create a rich and satisfying life for yourself and your loved ones?" is that there are people in your life that you love and care about. Not everyone is so lucky. If you are truly alone, your focus will be narrower than someone who has others in their lives. Narrower is not worse. It is not better. It's just different. Accepting this—and so many of life's other realities—helps you to deal with life in a calmer and more effective way. It is a habit you can form. And it is a key to genuine happiness.

These assumptions may not apply to you today. But if you continue reading and considering the possibilities for your life, my bet is that they will. I'll even go so far as to say they hold important stores of energy, which you will need to create your life of beauty and substance.

The last big question to consider is "What contribution do you want to make?" For many women, this question is a throwaway. For generations, women have been expected to contribute certain things like children, some form of beauty, grace, caretaking and nurturing qualities. An unusual woman might have been lucky enough to discover something new or invent something that has commercial value. But these contributions were expected more of men.

Notice the past tense. Today, women are encouraged to reach for the stars, go for the gusto, dream big dreams, and find a way to make them happen. That's a good news/bad news deal. The good news is that many constraints have been removed. The bad news is that there is precious little in the way of practical mentoring or encouraging or support that goes along with the ideal. Competition is more the order of the day than collaboration or cooperation. This should be no surprise when you remember that sadness you feel when you think someone else is luckier than you. If you feel your life has been unfair, the sadness may turn to anger or, worse, despair. This book will help you find a healthier, happier, more productive way forward.

> *Beware that you do not lose the substance by grasping at the shadow.*
> - Aesop

Becoming a woman of substance takes effort. And time. And a steadfast focus on the outcome you desire. It means turning off the media-hyped images of beauty and success. It means growing content with yourself and the way you are made. Becoming a woman of substance means discovering and embracing what my grandpa wanted to know: what you're made of.

Isn't this a far more interesting and exciting way of looking at your life than gazing into the mirror each morning and feeling dismay at the newest pimple or wrinkle?

Backbone: Your Key to Happiness

What does it mean to have a backbone? It means to stand up, speak up, make a decision, and take action. It means to know who you are, what you believe, and what you want. It means to be strong. Courageous. Principled.

This can be tricky business, especially if you are a woman. When you display a backbone, chances are someone will tell you what you are not: "You are not my mother!" or what you are: "What a bitch."

In my original book, *How to Grow a Backbone: 10 Strategies for Gaining Power and Influence at Work*, I identified the three elements that make up backbone: competence, confidence, and risk taking. These form a learning system that can be employed every day in working toward something that matters to you.

In my painful beauty pageant example above, I spent a lot of time trying to become competent as a dancer. I took a risk that, while not earth-shaking, was certainly very public and, as it turned out, pretty embarrassing. And somewhere deep inside I knew, even as I practiced, this was a mistaken undertaking. Still, having committed to the event and being too stubborn and scared to change course along the way, I couldn't see any alternative but to proceed as planned.

What I didn't know then and could only understand looking back from a distance is that it was one step toward building competence and gaining confidence in making personal choices. Hearing and listening to that tiny warning voice inside is a skill that we would all benefit from learning and trusting very early in our lives! Turns out I had a zillion other experiences and a lot of years of second-guessing before I finally understood I had not only the ability but also the responsibility to make good personal choices. Growing a backbone can take awhile.

My friend, Alison, had her eye on a big promotion at her law firm. She worked long hours, recognizing that in the legal profession time in the office is still a benchmark of dedication to the field. Alison got very good at being there. She also took the occasional risk of adding her voice to a discussion, usually by sparring with the men about football and baseball games. She would make a controversial pick to win a game and then enjoy sports banter with the guys.

However, Alison's confidence hovered at a low level with regard to the promotion she craved. She was careful in her work and rarely spoke without knowing the right answer. She often deferred to men in professional discussions, even when she knew her idea or comment would benefit everyone. Why? She did not want to jeopardize her chances at promotion by making a visible and potentially costly mistake. She developed strong competence in cautious behavior, which came across as uncertainty and a lack of confidence. Not the basis on which promotions are granted!

With a few minor changes, some practice and growing self-awareness, Alison developed new competence, which boosted her confidence. She recognized that the good-natured sports bantering she did with the men gave her a measure of acceptance and credibility with them. If she could talk football—and endure the sometimes coarse language that came with it—she might be trusted to hold her own in a tense legal debate.

Alison learned to appreciate the certainty she felt within the office environment. The time she spent there afforded her a sense of comfort and predictability. To the extent possible, she arranged to host challenging debates on her turf. That's called home field advantage.

Alison also kept track of situations in which she was welcomed and those in which she felt ignored or dismissed. She thought about the specific things that created her feelings and began to investigate the stories she told herself in each case.

Women often respond to the behaviors and feelings of others, even when those behaviors and feelings have nothing to do with them. We'll talk more about this later, but it is something to be aware of.

With growing competence comes increased confidence. As you get better at things, you feel a stronger sense of comfort and sureness. Of course this takes time! Trial and error is still a magnificent way of learning what works for you and what doesn't. Keeping track of your experiences, the feelings they evoke and the lessons you learn is a trusty way to get to know yourself. Trial and error also builds substance, which is essential to a grounded sense of self and a purposeful life. This confidence is steeped in experience not wishful thinking. This is the confidence that leads you to take intentional purposeful risk as you build your life.

Of course, backbone can be created just as easily by accident or making big messes. In fact, that's the way a lot of us learn. Take my friend, Barbara. Barbara is what you might call a black sheep—someone whose choices and behavior are considered unsatisfactory, even disgraceful, by family and members of the community.

From good-girl days as a youngster to rebellious episodes as a young adult, Barbara not only colored outside the lines, she threw the approved coloring book out the window! As a teenager with a weight problem, she was sensitive to the catty comments made by so-called friends and naturally disappointed that the coolest guys never looked her way. Adolescent hormones did nothing to help her think clearly and every perceived slight lashed at her confidence.

To compensate for hurt feelings, she ate. Potato chips by the bag, donuts by the box, ice cream by the quart, mint cookies by the dozen. Does any of this sound familiar?

As her weight soared, Barbara's feelings about herself plummeted. Although she was an outstanding student, she was not able to take pride in her grades because she was disgusted with herself physically.

As a young adult, Barbara entered into an abusive marriage. For several years, she cried each time she was beaten. But she hid her tears, bruises, and shame. She did not want anyone to know the truth of her situation; she feared their judgment. She did not want to appear weak or stupid or otherwise deficient. It was not until she gave birth to her first child that Barbara decided to find a way out.

Determined to protect the baby from her husband's violent abuse, she divorced him. The stigma of single parenthood seemed less burdensome than a lifetime of trying to protect her child. Some years later, Barbara became pregnant again. She knew she would not marry the father and she did not have the financial means to care for another child. Despite her religious upbringing and personal revulsion with abortion, she made the decision to abort.

Barbara's challenges and triumphs are many. She overcame an addiction to prescription drugs, another disastrous marriage, and years of alcohol abuse. She says her greatest victory as she looks back is the ability to forgive herself, even when others haven't been so kind.

In some ways, Barbara's story is every woman's story, albeit with far more drama than most of us encounter. It encompasses private struggle, public disapproval, and a stubborn determination to find her way. The self-acceptance she has found as a result of her many travails makes her a woman of tremendous beauty and substance today.

Notice there are no rich uncles, pathways strewn with rose petals, or violins playing in the background. Her life has been filled with adversity. Is she angry or looking for someone to blame? No. In fact, she says she would have it no other way. Yes, she regrets the people who were hurt along the way. To the extent she has been able, she has apologized and asked for forgiveness.

But the things she has learned about herself and the strength she has developed have filled her with gratitude, patience and tremendous compassion. Barbara grew a backbone the hard way!

I happen to love grown-up black sheep. Not because they act outrageous, but because they have experienced the damning judgment of others by making bad choices, following the wrong crowd, or doing something outside the lines of acceptability and gotten over it.

In the process of getting scuffed up by life, they have come to understand that what is inside matters more than what is outside. The resiliency they discover in the face of their travails, the capacity they uncover in bouncing back from mistakes, and the clarity they find in discovering who will stand by them in their hour of need are gifts of black sheep-ism that they cherish.

Whatever pathway your life takes, know that a strong backbone is your key to happiness. It lies in discovering who you become and what you contribute, not in how you look or what you acquire. This is a powerful, liberating key.

CHAPTER TWO

AN INTEGRATED PLAN
FOR A VERSATILE WOMAN

"Toto, I've a feeling we're not in Kansas anymore." So said Dorothy to her beloved pet. And so it is today.

The world you live in is very different than the world in which your mother and grandmothers grew up. That's not headline news, of course, but you may be surprised at how things have changed. Once upon a time, a woman's role was almost entirely prescribed by external rules. Based on traditional roles and responsibilities of husbands and wives, expectations were clear, and commitments made in marriage vows were sacrosanct.

A "good" woman was faithfully married—or chastely awaiting such good fortune—a churchgoer, a tender of family and community, and the supporter upon whom her family relied.

("Bad" girls wore outrageous clothes, used bad language, had questionable morals and were mostly shunned, except by bad boys and rogues who enjoyed their rambunctiousness.) The rock of the family was the husband. A woman's status in the community was largely determined by her husband's employment and her children's good performance in school. A "good" woman was personally modest: careful in attire and temperate in behavior. While your mom or grandma may not have liked these expectations—indeed many women chafed against them—she understood them. Consequently, her plan was fairly straightforward. Of course this is a gross over-simplification, but for a lot of women, life followed a closely written script.

Not so today!

Today's woman defies categorization. She has a dizzying number of choices and is expected to make sound decisions about everything from family to career to community service to social engagements, often with little support and always in the context of a very noisy society. Traditional values are still important, yet women feel more empowered to challenge traditional roles. Women who have grown up outside any religious affiliation tell me the values and even roles may be good, but the dictation of them is outrageous.

Today's woman is also a multi-tasker extraordinaire, especially when she is deeply involved in and excited about life's abundant opportunities. Sometimes, however, this multi-tasking is a result of feeling responsible for taking care of others first and self last. When this happens, resentment and frustration can drain positive energy in a hurry. Sorting through conflicting social and business directives can be exciting and paralyzing!

A Word About Roles, Choice and Compulsion

What is a woman's role in society today? This question, when posed in workshops, always triggers an animated discussion. Should she stay home with her children? Seek promotion at work? Explore careers in any field that interests her? Aspire to a Hollywood career? Run for high political office? Yes, yes, yes, yes, and yes. Choice is of prime importance, women say. Pay equity, shared responsibility at home, equal opportunity in higher office and the time to figure it all out are what they not only want, but expect.

Assumptions are uncovered; biases laid bare. Emotions run high. Women don't want to be pseudo-men. But they do want a shot at the power and money that men have. A woman should follow her dreams wherever they may take her, they say. Recognizing that reality will probably look quite different than her dreams gives them pause. Yes, she should also be mindful of the promises and commitments she has made.

> *Not only is women's work never done, the definition keeps changing.*
> - Bill Copeland

A woman's role in society has certainly expanded. There are many more choices today than our ancestors might have ever imagined. This is a good thing. It is also a challenging thing. What is a woman's role? How should we define—or redefine—femininity? How, indeed. However you answer that question, the responsibility you have for your life is complete. How you live as a woman today serves as a model for those who watch you. What are you teaching?

Women have always been caretakers, nurturers of children, keepers of the hearth. As opportunities expanded in educational institutions and the workplace, women got out to play in those arenas, too.

According to the US Council of Graduate Schools, in 2012 for the fourth year in a row, women earned the majority of graduate degrees. They have been earning the majority of master's degrees since 1986.

In business, the US Department of Labor shows that women made up 60% of the workforce in 1999, a high point. In 2011, that was down slightly to 58.1%. Get this: in 2011 70.9% of moms with kids under the age of 18 were working. As opportunities opened up, women took advantage of them.

However. And this is a big however. Although things are changing, women still have the primary responsibility for home and family matters. All this new opportunity is often added on top of traditional roles, not necessarily in place of them. This challenges women in both practical and invisible ways.

Let's approach this question then from the viewpoint of relationships. Not relationships as in love pairings, but relationship as in related to, working within, or not alone. On the day you were born, you began a relationship with the world that surrounded you. Your awareness of the world was extremely limited, of course, but it expanded throughout your childhood and adolescent development. If you were lucky, your awareness continued to expand throughout adulthood. You are luckiest of all if it continues today.

This notion of continually expanding awareness makes some people very tired. They don't want to know what the rest of the world is doing; they have enough to do just to manage their own stuff, thank you very much. Practically speaking, that's sensible.

But in a global community, which is increasingly inescapable, you may no longer have the luxury of staying home on the porch. That is to say new and different people are moving in at work, at school, and sometimes in your neighborhood. Your relationship with new people and ideas will have a lot to do not only with your definition of self (who you are) but also with your level of confidence in living the life you want to live.

The very act of self-discovery requires backbone. The noise of the outside world is very powerful in shaping identity; the tiny voice inside has little support in finding its range. Young women seek role models in their mothers, teachers, other family members, and celebrity figures. Unfortunately, because celebrities get the lion's share of attention, they shape modern standards of beauty and behavior. And these are highly changeable!

As mentioned, women were once expected to be happy as givers and nurturers. Their satisfaction and pleasure had its roots in relationships and well-defined role expectations. Women knew what was expected of them. Their value was derived from their ability to help. Life skills such as cooking, cleaning, mending, doing laundry, shopping for groceries and other family needs, organizing calendars, managing home and school activities, nursing, and helping with homework were essential to her success and happiness. Additionally, the ideal—and thus expected—temperament included such attributes as sweetness, patience, empathy, understanding, a peacemaking orientation, and of course tenderness.

No wonder the women's movement rose up with such energy. We might wish to be so saintly, but this ideal was simply unrealistic and, as it turned out, unsustainable.

The world has exploded over the past several decades, spilling out new jobs, communities, and cultures for women to explore. At the same time, changing social mores have demanded redefinition of nearly every expectation we once took for granted.

Scientific advances changed absolute notions regarding family structure and biological clocks. And technological developments made housekeeping tasks of all kinds much easier. The kaleidoscope of life turned not once or twice but dozens of times at dizzying speed! What does the picture look like these days?

A woman's role is what she chooses to make it. She may decide to be a mother, with or without the assistance of a husband. Similarly, a woman's choice of profession is as open as her imagination. Careers once thought to be almost exclusively male are today wide open to women.

This is a good news/bad news proposition. As freedom of choice has expanded, so has the number and weightiness of decisions a woman must now make. Where a woman always had the choice to marry or remain single, this choice used to include or bar any thoughts of children and family. Where she once had a narrow slate of professional avenues to choose from, a woman now has an endless array of opportunities. Simplicity then, though not always attractive, certainly made decision making easier.

So while the world has become a woman's oyster, which is an old expression meaning the world belongs to you and you can get anything you want, many women worry about whether they are making the right choices not only in the short term, but also for the long run.

And thus a new economic boom was born! The livelihoods of tarot card readers, astrologists, numerologists, and other sooth-sayers have been enriched by this uncertainty. I say this with some facetiousness, but it is true. Similarly, psychologists, psychiatrists, and other mental health workers have seen their workloads increase as well. Why might this be? With so much choice, shouldn't women be ecstatic? With little negative judg-ment and virtually no stigmatism attached to any decision no matter how avant-garde, how can a woman feel badly about any of her decisions? With no compulsion to adhere to social norms of the past, why would any woman feel regret or remorse if things don't turn out quite the way she expected?

Why indeed. The fact is that women are still very other-oriented. We still care about people. We want to be in relationship. We feel compelled to help people in need and satisfy expectations of our loved ones. As a mother and grandmother, I hope we never lose this concern because if women abandon it, we're all in serious trouble. What, then, is a woman to do?

A wise woman wishes to be no one's enemy;
A wise woman refuses to be anyone's victim.
- Maya Angelou

For now, recognize that no matter what your current circumstances are, opportunities exist for you to be better, stronger and happier. When you have a solid sense of who you are and what you want to do with your life, you are in a much stronger position to make choices for yourself and those you care about. You will also be better equipped to handle objection or disapproval from people who may disagree with your choices.

After what must have seemed like a hundred years of raising six kids, my mother decided to go back to school to earn a college degree and credentials as a medical technologist. Dad was ambivalent at best and of absolutely no help. In fact, he warned Mom that if things started slipping at home—if his mashed potatoes and gravy every night were threatened—there would be heck to pay. (Dad didn't swear.)

Though I had no idea then what a medical technologist was or the rigor of the training Mom was proposing to undertake, I had a very strong opinion about her decision. I was a teenager.

My youngest brother was in first grade and I believed that Mom's decision to focus on herself was selfish and wrong. I thought she was abandoning the family in important ways. I even blamed her for some of my brother's difficulties at school and with authority figures. Such moral clarity I had! And such a keen ability to judge others' decisions.

Fortunately, teenagers do eventually mature. My thinking evolved thanks to personal experience and I swallowed hard when my own words came back to me the first time I dropped my daughter off at daycare. I defended myself with the truth that I did not have the choice to be a stay-at-home Mom. I simply had to work to help pay rent and buy groceries.

Times change and the pendulum of possibility and expectation swings. We have discovered new territories for women while still feeling the pull of traditional values. This creates confusion and tension; much energy is expended in sorting things out. At some point the excitement of testing limits may be replaced with the question of just when you lost your mind.

Becca is a thoroughly modern mom and fantastically successful young professional. She has two children, a middle management position, a husband who works full time and a network of supporters from day care teachers to a professional organizer helping her manage her life.

Over coffee one afternoon, she spoke excitedly about a big project she was working on and the strong positive feedback she was getting from her employer. The people she had begun to meet came from all around the world and the places she visited helped her see a much bigger world than she had ever been exposed to before.

Becca reveled in this newness; she embraced the notion of becoming smarter, stronger, and more accomplished. She loved feeling like a major contributor to her family in terms of financial security and also as a leader in suggesting new places for the family to visit.

As she paused for a sip of coffee, her brow furrowed a bit. She swallowed, lowered her eyes, and stopped talking. A few seconds later, she started to shake her head ever so slowly side to side. Her hand went to her mouth and I watched her fight emotion and try to hold back tears.

I wanted to reach out. I wanted to ask, "What is it?" Instead, I sat quietly, waiting for her to speak or not as she felt ready. After several minutes, she reached into her purse, pulled out a tissue, and wiped away tears that had slid down her cheeks onto her chin. When she looked up again, her eyes were filled with pain and her face was convulsed in confusion.

"What's wrong?" I finally asked.

"My husband says he doesn't know me anymore. He says I've turned into the sort of ambitious woman he has always disliked. He told me I'm not a good mother."

At this point her silent tears burst into a sob.

Her worries spilled out in wrenching gasps. He has stopped hugging her, he doesn't look her in the eye anymore, and he skips bedtime stories with the kids. He seems preoccupied when they share meals together and he never laughs anymore. She wonders if he has found someone else or if he is satisfying his heretofore-healthy sexual appetite via the Internet. She is afraid to talk with him about it and angry with herself for this fear and hesitance. Rather than make time to sort things out in her own mind before deciding what to do, she plunges back into work or devises new ways to spend time with the kids.

Becca's story holds clues as to why many women feel that following their talent and listening to their heart is unrealistic. Growing in a career can be risky business, they say, especially when you have other responsibilities to family and friends who rely on you for support. Going one's own way is too lonely, too difficult, they say. Even in Becca's privileged, expanding life, isolation and sorrow found a place.

Must it be one way—your way—or the other way, preferred by people close to you? Must a woman go her own way in order to find happiness and satisfaction? Do you believe that other people are your adversaries who want to squash your dreams?

Your Interested Others

While you are deciding what role(s) you want to play and how you want your life to be, it's easy to lose sight of the fact that a number of others in your life may have an interest in what you're thinking. Your interested others might include spouse, partner, children, lover, co-workers, family members, business partners, committee co-chairs, neighbors or arch enemies. Caught up in your personal web of options and decisions, you may expect a level of attention and support that's bigger than the closest of these others can provide.

When this happens, you may end up hurt and they may feel like you're being unusually selfish or sensitive.

The fact of the matter is that people who love you do care about your happiness and generally want to help you achieve your dreams. The people who don't love you, but may be affected by your decisions, generally don't want to help you and probably hope they can throw sand in your gears. (Women with backbone are clear-eyed about this.) All are human beings with limited time, energy, perspective, and sometimes patience. When you decide it's time for a change, they may be deciding things are just fine the way they are.

Your interested others are not mind-readers! Women are notorious for expecting people who know and care about them to automatically know when they are working on something big. How many times have I heard, "If he/she loved me, he/she would know!" Don't do that. It's not fair and it makes people crazy.

Telling people that you're working on something important can be difficult. Dreams are fragile, especially in early stages, and your tendency will be to protect your dream while expecting support. We'll explore this in the last chapter, but suffice for now to say that communication is a challenge when your thoughts are fluid, your ideas change frequently, and you're still figuring out how to be a woman of beauty and substance.

It's funny, too, to recognize that you really like your interested others when they are on board with your plans and actively supportive of your efforts. These are smart, handsome, beautiful people! But let them question what you're thinking or doing and see how fast they become mean, ugly creeps who lack imagination and intelligence!

Julie left a cushy corporate job at the top of the pay scale to open a women's boutique selling unique and distinctive fashions. All during the planning stages, her husband, Randy, was her biggest cheerleader. When the boutique opened, Randy could be heard around town calling it a darling shop. He learned to say "unique and distinctive style" to his friends without smirking or feeling goofy. He wasn't embarrassed at all to distribute her business cards and special-offer postcards at community centers and Rotary meetings. Julie was thrilled to be married to such a wonderful man.

Fast forward one year. You would swear Julie is married to a completely different person. Julie says that Randy has not only stopped promoting her shop, he is now a complete ogre, constantly badgering her about advertising and inventory expenses. He asks about sales figures to mock and ridicule her, and he never takes her promotional materials to any of his meetings. Julie is now married to a jerk.

Randy is befuddled at Julie's ire. He admits to being less active in promoting her business, as challenges in his job require his attention. He figures that after a year, the boutique is well enough known in town it doesn't need his constant salesmanship. He also admits to being concerned about monthly sales and the cost of inventory. He understands that new fashions are essential to keeping the interest of patrons, but believes a more disciplined process of selection would benefit the business. Randy only wants what is best for Julie. He remains committed to her success.

The point here is that your choices impact others. Sometimes a lot of others. You can see how powerful resistance to a woman's change can be. You may believe that the best life for your interested others is having you stay just the way you are. They know what to expect from you and they know how to cajole or coerce you into doing things for them, whether you wish to or not.

Marcus Aurelius, 1st century Roman emperor, wrote: "The first rule is to keep an untroubled spirit. The second is to look things in the face and see them for what they are." Sage advice.

When you spend time developing a special talent or learning more about a subject or occupation that fascinates you, you become energized. You feel hopeful and happy because you can imagine your future being different than your present day.

What if you shared this energy and excitement with those who currently share your life? What if you could quietly begin to build a new future, not looking for either permission or validation? What if you could be strong enough to allow others to experience their discomfort with change without feeling the need to assuage it or make them wrong for feeling it?

You may be shaking your head thinking in your case this is simply not possible. If I understood what you were dealing with, I wouldn't even suggest this. I have heard this from many women; I have said it to myself at times. But I know from experience and personal testimony from a growing number of women that you can shape your life in a way that makes you happy. You don't have to fight with others in the process.

Yes, it may be true that those closest to you may want you to stay exactly as you are. But ask yourself, do your loved ones prefer a lethargic, depressed, angry or combative you over an energized, determined, accepting, happy you? Truth is, until you try a new way, you cannot know the answer.

Getting out of your comfort zone is a scary thing. It is best to start small, accept the responses of others as valid for them, and keep moving forward. Our work with women in Backbone Bootcamps has proven dramatically that you can have a powerful positive impact on the people who are most frightened of your growth.

Start small. Take time to capture moments, events, and projects that quicken your pulse or bring a smile to your face. These don't have to be just happy accidents of life. You can seek them out and create them on purpose. You can build a life around them, one activity at a time. Just like getting your muscles toned if you have never worked out or if you have been a couch potato for years, you start slowly and get into a rhythm, a habit of exercise.

Training yourself to behave in stereotype-busting ways is no more complicated. And it's no easier. It takes determination, continual effort, and conscious attention to—and assessment of—the results you are creating.

Keep a journal. Record your thoughts. Make note of things that capture your attention, and why. A popular exercise is to keep a gratitude journal. This was a life-saving exercise for me when my daughters were little and I was a single working mom. I looked back at this journal recently and could only shake my head when I saw page after page, day after day, these words: "We made it through this day." That was the thing I was most grateful for.

From today's perspective, I wonder: "Is that the only thing I could come up with?" Closing my eyes to re-consider those times, I remember the fatigue and fear that laced so many days. The uncertainty of whether I was doing the right things or teaching the right lessons. I remember feeling frantic at those questions. I was surviving! I simply had no leftover energy to find reasons for gratitude. Still, I did the exercise.

Later in the journal, I wrote: "Jenny's laughter sounds like bubbles of sunshine." "Kelly didn't have a stomach ache today." "My flight arrived home on time." Tiny fragments of life that we take for granted are captured in that journal. How grateful I am to have it today.

More recently, I started keeping a journal of "Things I Noticed Today." Many of the entries are observations of nature. The work of an ant. The presence of fireflies. A neighbor's tree that looks like a dandelion waiting for someone to make a wish and blow it away.

There are new observations of people I have known for a long time. The way this person closes his face when he is thinking, removing all expression from his eyes and facial features.

"Great Poker Player," I wrote. The way another person sounds on the phone when she doesn't really have much to say but wants to be distracted from whatever she was doing.

I notice that I do not bother to record ugly things.

Anticipating Life's Chapters

It's the same old question: Can women have it all? Depending on who you listen to, you'll feel hopeful of having it all and happily so, disgruntled because you cannot have it all—at least not easily or on terms you find acceptable—or completely frustrated because other women do seem to have it all while you do not.

May I ask: What does 'all' mean to you? If you made a list of everything you need to 'have it all' and be completely happy, what would be on it? People? Money? Art? Travel? Clothes? Jewelry? Cars? A mansion?

Now let me ask what you are willing to do to obtain all those things? Marry the richest person you can find? What if that person turned out to be a miserly grouch?

More questions. How much time would you expect to invest in maintaining your beautiful things? Paying taxes on them? Defending yourself from others who would envy or hate you because of your wealth? How much time would you have to truly enjoy having it all?

It doesn't look quite so awesome when you think about these things.

Here's the truth. You can have as much as you want if you are willing to do what is necessary to obtain the things you desire, whether that means marrying someone of means, working hard, investing wisely, or finding someone to get them for you by whatever means necessary.

Life unfolds in chapters. Think back to your elementary school days. What you wanted then changed by the time you got to high school and probably changed again after graduation. What you desire and aspire to as a teenager develops into something different—and usually more—by the time you reach your mid-20s, 30s and beyond. Gail Sheehy's books *Passages* and *The New Passages* outline these in some detail.

Expectations have changed and it is true we expect a lot more in far shorter time frames than ever before. This saddens me sometimes as I watch people become consumed with having stuff and losing so much in the process including their health, friendships, confidence and happiness. Not everyone, of course. And not always. Still, I wonder what is worth all that loss?

It is difficult to have patience when you are living a chapter that is frustrating, slow to develop or downright painful. Each stage of life has its challenges and rewards; I believe all are necessary to becoming a fully developed woman of beauty and substance.

Think of your favorite novel or movie. If every chapter or scene was sunshine and butterflies, you would be bored silly. If your favorite character did nothing but smile and scatter daisies, you would think the writer of the story inane. Every story has ups and downs, happy times and dreadful times. The best stories have epic struggles! Our favorite characters learn the most about themselves during dreadful times.

The same is true for you. You are writing your story, living the scenes of your life as they unfold. When life requires you to focus all your energies on survival or recovery, the frivolous fades away. During these times you discover your strengths and tap into your latent resilience. I have often wondered why we don't appreciate this more? Probably because we like to move through difficulties as quickly as we can and once past them, we don't like to think about them. That's too bad. Without fully appreciating your ability to cope, you lose the opportunity to intentionally build substance.

As you look ahead to what life might hold, your biggest questions may revolve around relationships, careers, and family. Impatience is not your friend. You may see opportunity and jump on it before thinking about what you want. This can make life a lot of fun and certainly interesting, however it can also lead to dead ends. I personally don't think any experience is wasted if you learn from it, but that's tough to remember when things don't work out as you hoped they would.

> *It takes courage to grow up and become who you really are.*
> - e.e. cummings

As life continues to unfold, your responsibilities tend to increase. You may choose to have a family, which will put new and different demands on you. You may choose to pursue advanced degrees, seek promotions at work, or get involved in political or civic endeavors. Anticipating that life will change in both predictable and unpredictable ways will help you cope when the dark chapters arrive.

A woman of beauty knows that her physical appearance will change. Dewy skin, clear eyes, and a toned physique will gradually give way to wrinkles, fog, and droops. It's a bummer that can turn into serious depression if you place your value in your looks. But what disappears in one arena can appear in another. If you work to gain wisdom while your body is changing, you will have a deeper more lasting beauty to share forever.

Think of it this way. When you have a heavy heart or find yourself in a serious jam, would you rather turn to a gorgeous ingénue for help or find a woman of greater experience and depth? How will you become this woman of experience and depth, who will be a source of wisdom and comfort for people you love?

Flexibility and Authenticity

Are you flexible in the face of quickly changing circumstances? Can you move freely from one course of action to another? Are you comfortable making new decisions based on new information? Can you re-imagine your life when something you wished for proves either unlikely or downright impossible to happen?

This ability to adapt is highly prized in a world that changes rapidly and sometimes unpredictably. Take a look at business for just one example. Once upon a time, getting a good job meant staying with the same employer from your first day until retirement. Indeed, having too many jobs on a resume was a bad thing. Potential employers considered a long list of jobs as evidence of some sort of character flaw such as lack of commitment, inability to perform consistently, or worse. The opposite is true today.

A 2010 study done by the American Bureau of Labor Statistics reported that for the thirty years between 1978 and 2008, Americans aged 18 to 44 held eleven jobs, with men holding slightly more than women. It also showed that earnings growth was more significant in younger years and that advanced education equated to more promotions. So frequent movement is no longer a black mark on your resume, especially if you can show advancing responsibility and salary.

What was once labeled flighty is now honored as flexible.

Karen is a human resources professional who has experienced this shift in attitude. She recounts a story from the mid-90s in which her company was looking for a senior level marketing executive. The woman they hired had a resume that read like a Fortune 500 *Who's Who*. One year here, eighteen months there, another year yet someplace else. Because the companies were all well-known, the president of her company thought the candidate must be smart and accomplished to have landed jobs at such premier companies. When Karen voiced caution because of the short duration of the candidate's employment each time, the president brushed her concern aside. He wanted his company's name to be added to the list of big guns already listed.

They hired the woman, touting her flexibility and having great expectations for her success. Care to guess what happened? She lasted just over two years. While employed, she traveled extensively, negotiated partnerships that made little sense, and otherwise demonstrated a woeful lack of understanding of the company's business and an even greater lack of concern. Karen's concerns were validated, but too late.

Today's employment picture looks much different. A long list of previous jobs, while still troublesome to some employers, holds much less stigma than it used to. Rapid advances brought by technology and globalization have forced equally rapid adaptation among workers. The ability to elevate your skills or learn completely new ones matters more than how many times you have done it. Performance is king. Substance matters.

Which brings us to the question of authenticity. When you feel pressure to adapt on a frequent or continual basis, it can be hard to find and hold fast to your core. It's one thing to be challenged at work; it is something else entirely to be pushed and pulled by a society celebrating first one type of person and then another.

As you gain confidence in your abilities, clarity in your desires and goals, and experience in dealing with things that don't play out the way you hoped, your level of authenticity will deepen. It will take time. It will be messy. It is worth your best effort.

CHAPTER THREE

ESTABLISHING A PRESENCE

Y_ou've seen her: the woman who walks into a room and without uttering a word captures the attention of nearly everyone. She's not drop-dead gorgeous, but she is neatly dressed. Some people know who she is; others are curious to find out. The first thing you notice about her is the energy she exudes. She is smiling, but not broadly. Her eyes are clear and bright. She

stands tall but appears totally relaxed. She reaches out with a smile to shake hands and say hello.

Is she a politician? A celebrity? A newswoman? No, she is the owner of a small business, a member of the local Chamber of Commerce. Her kids go to the town high school. She is a regular member of the community, just like you and me. But she shines somehow.

That gift of shining somehow is what we call *presence*. No matter where she goes, people notice this woman.

Contrast this with the flamboyant exuberance of another local businesswoman. Her laughter is boisterous; her gestures big and bold. She moves rapidly around a room, high-fiving some, skirting around others, always quick with a joke or a slightly off-color remark. She is a force of nature! Some people know who she is; others are either curious or not interested in finding out. What's the difference? Is it mere style?

Taking Your Place with Grace

There are many ways to make an entrance. Regally, with head held high, facial features controlled, and back in a straight upright line. You can come in like a bull in a china shop, all kinetic energy with little concern for who or what else is already there and no discernible path from entrance to exit. You can schlep into a room; shoulders rounded, eyes down, feet shuffling along. You can come in like a breath of fresh air, happy, light on your feet, smiling and speaking softly. You can march in and pause, waiting to be noticed. There are many variations on the theme.

The way you enter a room, engage with others, share your point of view and make room for others to share theirs are often matters of personality and upbringing. You learned by watching the way other people did it. If you were encouraged to express yourself, you will. If not, you probably won't. At least not much.

Taking your place is different than merely showing up. Taking your place with grace is special. The dictionary definition of grace is beauty or charm of form, composition, movement or expression. It is the perfect description of what a woman looks like when she arrives with a purpose in mind and a contribution to make.

In the first chapter, we talked about the uniqueness of beauty—you are one of a kind—and how beauty creates connection. When you prepare to take your place, what is happening in your mind directs how you will make your entrance.

Believing you are beautiful in your unique way allows you to feel proud of yourself. Having a reason to go where you are about to go gives you confidence. Knowing what you want to accomplish when you get there gives you a purpose. When you are prepared in this way, you look and sound different than when you simply show up someplace hoping for the best.

Nowhere is this more evident than at networking events or social mixers. Everyone knows that if you want to expand the number of people you know—and who know you—you must attend these gatherings. Funny thing is, most people check with friends or business associates they already know to see if anyone is going. They want a pre-made safety net in place just in case they don't meet anyone. Which of course is the reason why they go in the first place.

A lot of people admit to enduring such get-togethers for the sake of seeing and being seen. Their thinking is that if enough people see them at enough places, they will become familiar enough that someone will strike up a conversation. It's funny to see how often this happens.

Networking aside, before you can prepare to take your place you have to decide where that place is. Maybe it's as a speaker on a panel. Maybe it's a new business group. Maybe it's introducing yourself to a coffee group that meets regularly in your neighborhood. Maybe it's taking your place at a new job or after a promotion. Deciding where your place is can be challenging for women. Private internal questions pop up about what you deserve, what is appropriate, or what other people might expect of you. You may worry about not doing it right. You may not realize it, but other people worry about you, too.

Having grown up with brothers and working with mostly men in the early stages of my career, I know that when women enter a predominantly male environment, the guys are uncomfortable. They feel like they have to act differently—be more careful with their words, scratch more discreetly, and control the urge to belch. Sorry for those dreadful stereotypes, but they typify some male behaviors that men recognize they need to manage when women are around.

I got a hilarious earful of this stuff when I sat with my brothers and their friends around our family table as high school kids and listened to them talk. They didn't worry about me—I was one of the guys who could talk sports and play football in the street—but they did clam up when one of my girlfriends was present. It was funny to see and I teased them about it.

I noticed this in some of my early jobs, too. Men didn't seem to be particularly uncomfortable when I was around nor did they appear to make special accommodations for me. I did wonder once in a while how come I was invisible when they seemed to notice every other girl who passed them in the hall or sat in a meeting. "What's wrong with me?"

In my naiveté, I assumed that women could go pretty much anywhere they wanted and talk with anyone who interested them. Then I learned about the Glass Ceiling and the Old Boys Network. Women who didn't get promotions complained about the men who got them instead. They blamed the Glass Ceiling for holding them back and the OBN creeps who built it. It didn't make a lot of sense to me, but they sure were mad.

Sometime in the late 1980s I was introduced to Catalyst, a non-profit organization founded in 1962, whose mission is to expand opportunities for women and business. The organization is dedicated to getting women more connected to business and helping them advance. The company I was working for at the time had started looking seriously at the issue of equal employment opportunity and research from Catalyst helped us think about what to do.

We had more men than women in the company and virtually no women in senior executive positions. We were like a lot of other companies back then. As we studied our employee statistics and debated our options, the company decided to set informal quotas for hiring more women. I suppose like a lot of other privately held firms, our intentions were good, but we stumbled in trying to make them real.

More importantly, however, women stumbled in trying to make strong positive impressions both during the interview and on the job. The term "glass ceiling" became a bit of a refrain when anything went wrong. Mean old men who said they wanted their companies to be more inclusive, acted like they wanted any women they did hire to stay on the other side of some imaginary barrier and keep their ideas to themselves.

During that era, you could ask any stalled-out female executive why she had stopped getting promoted and she'd tell you in great detail about the glass ceiling. But the truth is such women were unprepared to take their place, with or without grace. Many felt they had to work twice as hard as men to prove themselves, which put an unattractive chip on their shoulders. A lot of them had children at home and pretty heavy expectations from their husbands about how clean the house needed to be or what time dinner needed to be on the table. Naturally, these husbands got lumped in with the Neanderthals of the Old Boys Network and life at home became part of the struggle for women to be valued properly.

I take this trip down memory lane for several reasons. First, to illustrate that women had to work hard to break into what had been almost exclusively male territory. They weren't always graceful in the process. Second, to say that things are easier in some respects for women today than they used to be. You may not believe that, but it's true.

Third, while we've come a long way, baby, there is still work to do. Finally, how you think about your current circumstances will have a big impact on how you take your place. In this regard, some things never change. And that's a wonderful thing because you have a giant say in getting where you want to go.

I often ask women in my workshops whether they believe the Glass Ceiling still exists. Many do. Maybe you do, too. I don't. Here's why. If there were truly a glass ceiling, we would not see female CEOs, women in senior management positions or in the boardroom, and we probably would not see women holding high offices in government, at universities or in major non-profit organizations. While you may contend there are too few women, the fact that there is a growing number suggests that the glass ceiling has dissolved or it is very porous.

If the Glass Ceiling still exists where you are, I'd like to ask you a question. Do you have a glasscutter? For me, it is football. Having grown up watching football with my grandpa, dad, and brothers, I learned the sport by asking dumb questions, following favorite players, and taking a loss by the home team way too seriously.

> *Be in your own*
> *skin as an act*
> *of self-love.*
> - H. Raven Rose

I even played quarterback once in a while and I'm proud to say I learned to throw a pretty tight spiral. Not far, mind you, but distance was less important in our ragtag street scrimmages than accuracy.

Developing this competence—and sticking with it over the years—has given me the confidence to talk football with almost anyone. Guys are impressed. While that's not my motivation for engaging in football banter, I do enjoy the camaraderie it provides.

Finding something you enjoy that the men you work with relate to and enjoy, too, is a natural, human way to connect. Whether it's sports or cooking or gardening or skin care (yes, men are increasingly interested in cosmetics), your glasscutter can help you find a way to take your place.

Taking your place with grace is all about understanding your talent, experience, goals and the availability of what you are looking for, then showing up for a discussion about same. Others may have a different opinion of your self-assessment and they are entitled to it. Keep your eyes on where you're going and your energy focused on moving forward.

Now, it is natural for anyone who has to alter his or her behavior in order to accommodate a newcomer to feel uncomfortable and a little irritated. To someone outside the circle, this discomfort can feel like closed ranks. Taking your place with all this silently going on can be tough. Doing so with grace may seem next to impossible, especially if you feel like the group should be more welcoming.

When you feel someone should be doing something they're not and you're negatively affected, your attitude sours. A bad attitude does not lead to grace. It's the Glass Ceiling/Old Boy Network trap. Don't go there.

Focus instead on some common sense things you can do to take your place wherever you want to be. Do your homework on that place. Find out who the players are. Find out what they care about. Figure out how what you know and who you are could be important to them. Then go check it out.

If you are newly promoted and joining a management team, chances are you know, and have preconceived ideas about, who these people are, what they do, and how they are likely to react to your arrival. Be careful about your assumptions as you take your place among them.

Antoinette, "Toni," was fast-tracked to a senior management role in her company. She is smart, politically savvy, and a proven producer; her promotion was well deserved. Toni was the second woman to join the executive team and felt some comfort in knowing a female colleague was already there. Little did Toni know, however, that this colleague had stirred the pot with regard to her promotion. She had primed some of the men to look at Toni as an aggressive, glory-seeking woman with little concern for anyone but herself.

The first several meetings felt strained and awkward for Toni and she noticed a couple of men seemed especially resistant to her input. She didn't say anything publicly, but kept private notes about the tone and temperature of the meetings. Several months after her promotion, she approached her female colleague, hoping to share her concerns and ask for advice on how to better acclimate to the executive team. The woman told her she was imagining things and being over-sensitive, which can only be expected from someone less experienced. Toni dismissed her somewhat condescending tone and decided to take the woman's advice not to worry; things would eventually straighten out.

Eventually, one of the men who knew what Toni's colleague had done told her. Toni was shocked, angry, hurt and embarrassed. Her thoughts turned almost instinctively to retaliation or some way to expose the woman for her wickedness.

That's a natural response, but it is not useful. What Toni came to understand is that even when you are proud to take your place, not everybody wants you there.

Similar stories could be told about friends, neighbors, car pool ladies, and dozens of others. Being clear about your assumptions can help you head them off at the pass or minimize ill effects.

As a newcomer to any group, you will be a bit of a novelty. Expect to be inspected. You will be asked a lot of questions and some people may look at you too directly or for too long. While this may feel creepy, it is normal. Take it in stride. Politely answer questions you are comfortable with; turn away from gawkers. If someone asks you for information that is too personal or simply none of their business, practice saying with a smile, "Now that's an interesting question that I am not going to answer." When you can draw boundaries with assurance and a touch of humor, people will understand very quickly that you are a person of substance with whom they would be fortunate to associate.

A note of caution: The line between assurance and arrogance can be a fine one, and humor can sometimes be misunderstood. Practice with friends and associates until you feel comfortable being quizzed and setting boundaries. Remember that people who like to embarrass or put others down are often immature or insecure; don't give them fuel by over-reacting to their boorish behavior. While you may not be able to avoid these people entirely, you can limit your time with them.

This practice of taking your place with grace starts with a mindset. You are an interesting woman with a perspective on life that is different from anyone else's and just as valid. An attitude of curiosity is helpful when encountering a new group, as is a sense of humor as previously mentioned. Respecting that there is a history that precedes you allows you to ignore slips of the tongue or lapses in behavior. It also helps you recognize unspoken roles and rules within the group that are important as you learn to navigate within it. Missing these can lead to trouble.

Lanier is a former executive who took time off in her late 30s to raise two children. While out of the paid workforce, she volunteered for several community non-profit agencies, serving as committee chairwoman for a major fundraising event that drew business and government dignitaries from around the region. Lanier was smart, assertive and hard working; she quickly made a name for herself. She met lots of people, was involved in important policy discussions, and generally considered herself a player in the non-profit world. As a result, she rarely asked permission to be invited to the table, she simply showed up.

Her boldness in assuming she was welcome anywhere she wanted to go rubbed some important people the wrong way. You can guess what happened. Lanier was gradually brushed aside. Over time, she got less information from fewer people, which made her more aggressive in trying to find out what was going on. Lanier knew how to take her place, all right. She didn't know or understand the grace part.

In summary, women who know why they are taking their place, believe they have something of value to contribute, and are sensitive to what's going on with others are more likely to be accepted in any group. Here are some questions to ask yourself as you consider stepping into a new job, a new role, or a new environment:

- **What do I bring to this?** What accomplishments fortify your confidence and which of them would add cache to the group?

- **What do I want out of it?** Business connections, new friendships, a potential love interest?

- **Who is already here and what do I know about them?** What sources do you consult? What history do you have with certain members?

- **What preconceived notions might they have about me?** How do you know? What sources do you consult? How trustworthy are they?

- **What preconceived notions do I have about them?** (Be honest.)

- **How do I want them to perceive me and how can I create this impression?** Trying too hard is a common mistake. Take it easy. Be yourself.

- **How will I deal with people who want to make me uncomfortable?** Anticipating that some people may be rude lets you take it in stride if it happens.

Doing your homework in an objective, practical way and allowing time to check out your assumptions will provide a solid foundation upon which to take your place with grace.

Looking the Part You Want to Play

Costumes define characters in our favorite movies, plays and sitcoms. They do in life, too. A businesswoman is typically dressed more formally than a sports fan. A mom's everyday attire probably looks a bit more casual than a real estate agent's. Teachers wear different clothing than aviation mechanics. If you go to church, you probably wear a different outfit than when you're pulling weeds in the garden.

The question of clothing can be challenging, especially since our ideas about what is appropriate shift so often! Should you wear the latest styles by recognized designers? (Assuming you can afford them.) How expressive should you be with your choice of clothing? What about accessories?

The best clothing choices are made with respect for specific circumstances including institutional traditions, the level of physical exertion you anticipate, and the likely clothing choices of people you'll be with.

As you determine your personal style, please pay attention to your body shape and size, your age, the circumstances in which you expect to appear and your personal comfort with specific fabrics and fashions. What part do you want to play? Dress accordingly.

I'm a little embarrassed to confess this, but I remember going on an interview at an ad agency early in my career. The agency was famous in the area; their clients were among the best known nationally. I applied for a job as copywriter, feeling bold in taking the step. Though I was confident in my writing skills, I had never set foot in an ad agency in my life. The account executives I knew and had worked with from various advertising agencies were always dressed in suits and ties. I assumed that was the norm.

Consequently, what I wore to the interview was absolutely wrong for the role. I wore a pastel suit, complete with long silk scarf and ridiculously high heels. I thought I looked quite smart. When I got to the agency, I found out that writers were typically dressed in jeans and tee shirts. Boy, did I feel dumb. Worse, I didn't get the job. I'm convinced one look was all it took.

That shook my confidence as far as fashion goes. Raising a couple of teenage girls didn't help. In fact, they conspired to protect me from embarrassing myself with two little words: *Should not.*

Whenever I came out of my bedroom in an outfit that didn't look right to them—or more accurately, would embarrass them should anyone find out I was their mom—"should not" sent me back to try again. Sometimes I let them help me; most times I put on something previously approved. Though we don't like the thought, it is true that people judge a book—you—by its cover. What you wear says a lot about what you think of yourself and how well you understand the part you want to play.

You'd be lucky to have a 'should not' police to help. Jeans, tee shirts and flip-flops generally don't represent you well in an interview. (The exception perhaps being an ad agency.) Similarly, dressing for the cocktail lounge on a normal workday can raise questions about your focus.

And then there's the question of body piercing and tattoos. This form of self-expression has blossomed over the past couple of generations and has generated tremendous dialog about what is proper at work. People serving the public are sometimes advised to remove piercings and cover tattoos. Professional offices typically dictate a quieter expression of personal style. Some of these preferences are driven by what customers or clients expect.

When these preferences conflict with your personal style, you have a choice in how you respond. You can decide these expectations are outdated or irrelevant to your work and choose to ignore them. This will bother some customers but not others. As such, your decision can serve as a filter, letting you screen out those who prefer to deal with someone more traditionally dressed. They may also serve as a filter to your employer. If your personal expression trumps compliance to a dress code, you may find yourself newly available to the industry. Which means looking for a new job.

You might decide to tone down your personal style while at work, which many women do. This choice comes with an acceptance of the reality of everyday work and allows you to express yourself differently at work, at home and at play. You can see this as a limitation or a way to learn about the various aspects of your personality and the flexibility with which you adapt to different circumstances.

Fashion designers push change; it's what they do. In the real world, you are usually better off erring on the side of modesty than flamboyance until you achieve a level of professional competence or personal credibility. You may not like this bit of advice, but consider the criteria upon which you want to be judged for the part you want to play. Is it the cover or the story inside?

Choosing Your Words and Your Moment

In the same way your choice of costume establishes a presence, so do your words. In fact, one of the surest ways to establish a reputation is with your speech. Whether you choose your words carefully and speak with a measure of discretion or let it all hang out, what you say, how you say it, and when you say it will make an impression that has the power to reinforce or cancel out the presence you have so carefully engineered.

One advantage of being an unknown entity as you set out to establish a presence is that you are, to a certain extent, a blank slate. People have not yet formed strong opinions of you, even if your reputation precedes you. What I mean is that if you are generally known as a certain kind of person because of how others talk about you, the real you has an opportunity to further that reputation or create a different one.

How you speak, how often, and when is a powerful tool at your disposal.

Claire has earned a reputation for being outspoken and direct, sometimes painfully so. She is the woman in the committee meeting who speaks loudly, plainly, and often. Her gestures are as big as her voice. When a group to which she had applied for membership turned her down saying she wasn't a good fit for them, she was stunned. In typical fashion, she set out to find out why. After being stonewalled by a number of women, she cornered a friend and demanded a truthful answer.

Claire's friend explained as gently as she could that Claire's style is perceived more often than not as somewhat aggressive, not terribly sophisticated, and sometimes overly boisterous. Take away the qualifying words and the truth is that Claire is aggressive, coarse and loud. She doesn't know how to tone things down or keep quiet.

Claire argues that she is just being authentic and the world needs more authentic people. There is too much playacting, she says. She considers herself a role model for women who are timid or overly constrained by rules, proudly showing them how to

stand boldly in their shoes and proclaim their point of view. In Claire's case, this is devoid of any sensitivity to others. Claire believes her friends accept her as she is and expects others to do the same. This expectation is wrong and it hurts her.

Claire's aggressiveness causes others to put up barriers to protect themselves. She does not understand this and frankly, judges those who do so to be weak. This judgment may or may not be accurate, but it helps to further her reputation, which is leading with greater frequency to closed doors.

> *The foolish and wicked practice of profane cursing and swearing is a vice so mean and low that every person of sense and character detests and despises it.*
> - George Washington

Melinda is the opposite of Claire. She agonizes over her words, is reluctant to speak without proper preparation and rehearsal, and would never offer a spontaneous opinion. Melinda believes that her point of view, though educated, is of minor significance when measured against her peers. She is so careful to choose exactly the right words that windows of opportunity for her to speak open and close rapidly. She is content to watch them do so. Melinda's boss tells her she needs to work on developing executive presence. Part of this work entails speaking more often, louder, and sometimes first.

Both of these women are challenged to establish a presence that is credible. Their stories also illustrate the difficulty in trying to define a presence that is accepted and admired by all. There isn't one. Decide where you want to be and use your speech to help you get there.

A quick word about coarse language. Inspired in part by a hyper-visible, celebrity-oriented world, some women seem to have bought into the notion that shock talk is good. Bold statements made with vulgar words capture attention and put them on the map. That's true. The question is for how long and to what end?

You may laugh at clever one-liners your favorite sit-com characters come up with and wish you could be so witty with friends and so sweetly devastating with foes. Sit-coms are not reality and even reality shows are overdone for the sake of entertainment. People in the real world don't have a cadre of writers preparing scripts for them. They do have real feelings.

Women of beauty and substance work on choosing words that connect people (remember beauty connects), foster appreciation for different perspectives (your beauty is unique and so is theirs), and lead to deeper understanding. Growing your vocabulary is an act of substance that simultaneously builds confidence. Choosing words that invite dialogue and encourage exploration creates an environment of collaboration.

Losing inflammatory expressions and stupid words like the "f-bomb" is a discipline worth working on. It can be tough if your circle of friends routinely puke them out, but your effort and energy toward cleaning up your language will go a long way toward enhancing your presence.

Drama Is Not Your Friend

We all know a drama queen. She is precious, sensitive, highly volatile, and a royal pain in the neck. There is no peace where the drama queen lives. It may appear that this woman gets what she wants while others don't, but it comes at a cost. Fact is, drama paves a certain and indisputable route to establishing a presence nobody wants to be around.

Diana is the oldest child in a large family, raised with high expectations and tremendous support. Diana's father taught her that she could do whatever she put her mind to. He championed her ambition, protected her from criticism and struggle, and told her often that she was his princess. Along the way, Diana learned that her father would come to her aid whenever she felt disappointed or hurt. She put all her trust in his strength and learned that her helplessness was the key to his support.

Imagine a little girl learning to ride a bike. You may remember your own journey down the bike path. The process involves tipping over, scraping knees, ankles and shins, and it usually requires a Band-Aid or two. If someone sees you go down and rushes to your side, freaking out about possible injury, you quickly begin to see a spill as far more important and dramatic than it would be if no one made it their personal emergency to see to your immediate welfare.

Done often enough, you learn that whenever you feel scared, hurt or embarrassed, all you have to do is scream, cry, or create a scene and someone will appear to soothe your fears and take away the imagined monster. This is extremely unattractive and no way for a woman of beauty and substance to try to establish a presence. Oh, you'll be noticed. But you won't be highly or respectfully regarded.

When Diana left the family nest and encountered a world that was nowhere near as loving, invested or impressed with her as her father had been, she was helpless on one hand and enraged on another. She demanded attention, support and restorative compensation for the tiniest inconveniences.

People learned with great haste to avoid Diana, not take her histrionics seriously, and restrict her exposure to people and situations that matter. What a shock to this woman who had been taught that she could go anywhere and do anything her incredible mind could envision.

The cost of drama is high. Not only do you pay a price in damaged credibility, you waste other people's time, distract their attention from more important issues, thus retarding progress, and ultimately become a liability to a group or organization. No one has time to soothe your overwrought ego. Besides, since when is your comfort more important than someone—everyone—else's?

Now some people are born with high intensity genes that generate tremendous amounts of energy. Lucky people, these. Learning to channel the energy appropriately can propel them to great heights. I'm not suggesting that any show of energy or emotion is drama. In fact, feigning drama is a technique used by some speakers to engage an audience quickly. This is quite different from practicing drama as a way to gain and hold attention. Telling a good story is effective. Trying to be the damsel in distress is not. When it is important to you to establish a presence that commands respect, drama is not your friend.

Katie disagrees with me wholeheartedly on this point. She tells me her husband loves it when she needs his help. He is her knight in shining armor and they both love it when he comes to her defense. He feels wonderfully masculine and she revels in her femininity. Fine. Make your personal life magic. Just don't expect the rest of the world to love and defend you like your husband does. The rest of us have too much to do to rush to your aid every time you're overwhelmed.

Paula is another who disagrees with my point of view on this. She is a petite woman with a voice that is more high-pitched than she would like. She argues that without being frequently vocal and sometimes using salty language she can't get anyone to listen to her, not even the family dog. Paula has made up her mind to use what she believes is necessary to be seen and heard. She forgets to ask herself, by whom?

What place do you want to take in your world? What role do you want to play? Use your appearance and speech to help you get there. If you need help, don't hesitate to reach out. Remember, a trusted "should not" cop can be a very good friend.

CHAPTER FOUR
ARE YOU SERIOUS?

I t's a funny thing about life: the harder you work to make people take you seriously, the more they look at you like you're nuts. Or like you have a problem they really don't want to know about.

It's hard when someone is screaming at you to try to understand her side of a story. Harder, still, to watch your boss make a face behind someone's back and expect to be respected.

When you are intent on having others take you seriously, you can be trapped into thinking you're more important than another. Or smarter. Or more accomplished or entitled. Or whatever. Remember Diana's story from the last chapter.

Of course, the flip side is true as well. You can get so caught up in what others think of you that you lose sight of your accomplishments.

Joanne stood at the entrance of the boardroom, nodding with satisfaction at the arrangements for her important meeting. Materials were carefully placed at each seat, refreshments neatly arranged on the sidebar, and technologies at the ready. She anticipated a successful meeting and looked forward to winning over new investors to her budding company.

Butterflies skittered inside her tummy, but she appreciated the extra boost of adrenaline they offered. She turned with a smile as people began to arrive.

Drop the idea that you are Atlas carrying the world on your shoulders. Don't take yourself so seriously.

- Norman Vincent Peale

Twenty minutes into the meeting, Joanne was broadsided with a question she had not anticipated. Caught off guard, she blinked, swallowed, and quickly searched the room for a friendly face. Finding none, she felt her mind go blank. Fearful of looking unprepared or inept, she felt the heat creep up her neck and into her face. She stammered an apology, said she would have to do some research, and changed the subject. For the rest of the meeting, she avoided eye contact and stuck closely to her scripted remarks.

When the session ended, attendees shook her hand and thanked her for a very productive meeting. She avoided looking them in the eye while offering stiff handshakes of thanks. She never got over the awkward moment; indeed, she felt deeply embarrassed by her lapse. As the last person left, Joanne burst into frustrated tears. How would these people ever take her seriously again?

This is a costly overreaction. The people at the meeting hold Joanne in high regard. Her work over time has consistently demonstrated her professionalism, concern for accuracy and quality, and keen mind. In short, they take her seriously. Her awkward response in one unexpected moment does not change this opinion. Everyone has moments like that. By holding on to her embarrassment and allowing it to stifle her thinking and actions going forward, Joanne runs the risk of damaging her stellar reputation.

Yours truly had one of those moments in a very public way. While speaking to an audience of 350 female pharmaceutical executives, I lost my train of thought mid-sentence. For several seconds, I simply looked at the audience, hands at my sides, trying desperately to remember what I was saying. Slowly, I raised an index finger and said, "That thought is going to circle around and come right back. So let's sit quietly for a moment until it returns."

In that moment of quiet, I had the big beat-me-up stick in hand and my inner critic was screaming at me. "How can you be so stupid?! Do you know who these ladies are? You are so DONE!"

Seconds later, I shrugged my shoulders and said, "Well, it is apparently going to take longer to come back than we have time to wait. So let's move on."

The audience roared and applauded. Who could not relate to that mental lapse? Who could not appreciate how yours truly must have felt standing on stage in bright lights before a group of successful women? (Beam me up, Scotty!) Bless them for appreciating the self-deprecating humor, which not only lightened the moment, but also served to bond us as we shared embarrassing moment stories over lunch.

Say What You Mean

In spite of the occasional mental block that stops us cold, women are talkers. We tend to think out loud and sometimes need to verbalize what is on our minds before we reach a conclusion about what we mean. Social scientists tell us that girls are socialized to be more verbal than boys. Singing and chatting during play are more common among girls. At least they used to be. Is this still true or is it a stereotype we are wise to challenge?

Turns out researchers in studies from 1988 through 2010 found that verbal performance between girls and boys is only slightly better among females. "The difference is so small that it appears that gender differences in verbal ability no longer exist."

> *The right to be heard does not automatically include the right to be taken seriously.*
> - Hubert H. Humphrey

So says the 1988 study "Gender Differences in Verbal Ability: A Meta-Analysis" sponsored by the National Science Foundation, Washington, D.C. and written by Janet Shibley Hyde and Marcia C. Linn. The study is 75 pages long, which ironically seems to make my point.

At any rate, my own observations over 30 years of working with individuals across a broad spectrum of industries, academics and non-profit organizations suggest that, in general, women talk too much. Some of the chatter is social, some is thinking out loud, and some is really important! It is the important stuff we want to capture and present in such a way as to positively impress listeners.

To do this, it is essential to identify what you mean to say. This can be devilishly difficult! Too often what you want to say gets buried under assumptions about what you're supposed to say, what others expect you to say, or what is appropriate to say. If you ever wanted to bring up the elephant in the room—a subject everyone knows needs discussion and resolution—you know exactly what I mean. It takes a brave soul to approach certain topics. Doing so without first knowing what you want to say is sheer foolishness.

Another aspect of this difficulty lies in the fact that most of us have been trained to speak from our roles rather than from our hearts and minds. What do I mean? Consider the way you meet new people. When asked to share something about yourself, you'll typically talk about your role at work, home, school or in the community. "I'm a new mom." "I am vice president of business development." "I teach third grade." "I train dogs."

While this may be interesting information, it doesn't really tell anyone who you are. "I love the fresh green of spring and veggie pizza." The tendency to speak in approved ways can be comforting; we know what to expect from one another. Indeed, sharing personal details can lead to people dismissing you as not serious! But when we live too long on a superficial plane, we lose the ability to know what we truly mean to say.

Ergo, the tendency to babble.

Jamie wants a raise. She has bills to pay, school to afford, and she needs a new car bad. In thinking about how to approach her boss, Jamie does her homework on salaries and pay grades for her kind of work. She talks to friends, recruiters, even a consultant who advises businesses on pay issues. As she gathers this information, she gets excited about having extra money. She dreams big. By the time Jamie sits down with her boss, she is so full of energy and ideas she can hardly contain herself.

Throughout her eloquent and informative presentation, Jamie forgets to mention one thing: the value she adds to her department and the company. Ultimately, that's the only thing her boss cares about. Because her boss likes her and values her work, he patiently instructed her to go back and think about her answer to that question. He then suggested they meet again the following week.

If you are presenting evidence to support a point of view or bolster a request, start by stating your point of view or request succinctly and with clarity. Offer headlines that support your position and be prepared to add fuller text as part of the discussion.

I know this feels risky. Laying your cards on the table can feel like you are handing power to the other person. Negotiating experts tell you that's folly. But we're not talking about adversarial power struggles here. We're talking about having the courage to say what you mean in a way that makes sense and honors the other person's ability to understand.

If you mean to let someone know their words or actions have rubbed you the wrong way, you need to be clear in your own mind what the words or actions were and why you found them offensive. On a crabby day, you might be irritated by a particular tone of voice that you would not so much as notice on a happy day. When you react to this tone of voice one day but not another, you confuse the person whose tone is sometimes objectionable. This lack of consistency is a major reason why women are not taken seriously.

So before you can say what you mean, you must decide what that is. Spending a few minutes in reflection can be a powerful way to sort through your thoughts and pick out the ones you want to share. Additionally, slowing down long enough to do this has a calming effect when you are agitated. The impact of saying what you mean can be a game changer. And you have to do it, you can't just think about it.

When you have said what you mean to say, *stop talking.* Please. Give people time to digest what you have presented. Let them respond when they are ready, not in a timeframe you demand.

This ability to stop talking takes practice. Most people are acutely uncomfortable with silence, especially when they are passionate about getting a particular answer. Watch a little kid try to convince his mom to buy a box of his favorite ice cream sandwiches. The kid doesn't shut up! A lot of those kids are now adults with no greater skill at being quiet. Don't be that kid.

It is tough to be taken seriously when you make so much noise with your mouth it's hard to recognize what you are trying to say. Think about your message. Pick the words that best convey it, remembering your audience. Say what you mean. Give the other person time to respond. I guarantee your status as a person to be listened to will rise appreciably.

Modulate Your Voice

An unfortunate characteristic of the female voice is that it tends to increase in volume and pitch as women get angry, excited, nervous or scared. These emotions have an impact on energy, which resonates in our voices.

Listen to an angry or excited woman. She speaks loudly and sometimes with an ear-piercing shrillness. A nervous woman can sound breathless. A scared woman may sound like she is choking. Incidentally, men's voices can be altered by emotion, too, but they tend to keep emotion in check more rigorously than women do. A pernicious stereotype? Perhaps, but it is a popular perception that defines, at least in part, your reality.

To be taken seriously, modulate your voice. When you are angry, force yourself to slow down. Breathe deeply for a moment or two. Think about what you want to say; write down a few key words then practice keeping your voice at a normal volume and pitch. Speak at a normal rate. Naturally in the heat of the moment this advice is about as useful as an umbrella in a hurricane. That's why it is important to practice away from the action until it becomes second nature.

The benefits you will gain from practicing voice modulation will spill over into other aspects of self-control with highly beneficial results. For example, when you can take time to investigate your anger, you may find that you sometimes over-react to someone's words or actions. Women tend to personalize things, a habit we will explore in the next chapter.

When you train yourself to speak in moderated tones, you may find that people no longer run screaming from you when you are angry. They will take your offense more seriously and may seek ways to mend fences. Yes, some may continue to act defensively, charging you with over-reacting. And some may take an offensive posture, challenging your credibility or the very reason for your anger. Be ready for it.

Rachel was indignant about the jerks in her office who always commented about the buxom NFL cheerleaders while discussing the weekend's football games. She thought they were pigs; they loved to get her goat. When they could send Rachel huffing and puffing down the hallway, they high-fived and went back to work.

Similarly, if they wanted to distract or diminish Rachel's input in meetings all they had to do was make a gesture or mention one of the cheerleaders and Rachel was off like a dog on a hunt. She hated that they did this and stubbornly refused to see her predictable participation. She also complained about not being taken seriously—especially by a bunch of juvenile co-workers. Oh, the irony.

Do What You Say

When you say you're going to do something, do it. This is a painfully obvious bit of advice, but one that seems increasingly difficult to follow. In our 24/7 world, it is not at all unusual to reschedule meetings, dinners, social events, and time at the gym. In fact, your workout may be one of the first casualties of an overcrowded calendar. My fitness routine fell apart entirely as I finished work on this book!

On the surface, this rescheduling is no big deal; it happens all the time. But when you look at what's really happening, you are not doing what you say. Sometimes it involves others; sometimes it's a private disconnect. Either way, it pings at your sense of self, which opens a doorway into allowing others to challenge your seriousness. Let me explain.

Informal polling of professional women's groups shows that multi-tasking and rescheduling appointments is a fact of everyday life. These women admit that they experience a near-constant state of movement and change that challenges their self-confidence. Unfortunately, they consider it normal to say something one day and do something else the next. And yes, they acknowledge that this tendency impacts other people in their lives. Trust becomes an issue.

This act of constant schedule shuffling begs the questions of priorities and purpose, which are difficult for many to answer. 'What is my purpose' is too big a question in the midst of a zillion things that need to get done today. Is it? Or might figuring out why you do what you do allow you to stop doing some things in order to do others better?

When everything is urgent and emergencies pop up daily, you have no priorities other than to react to what's happening around you. This can feel good! Having the answer to the big problem of the day and cleaning up a mess no one else is capable of handling grants you heroine status. You get things done!

You can see the snowball effect. Pretty soon bigger opportunities will blow by you because you are so busy. Which will make you angry and resentful. Which will get you talking too much to the wrong people. The end result is that you are taken less seriously than you want to be. What to do? Slow down. Think about what you mean, say it, then do what you say. Keep promises to yourself and others. When you take your commitments seriously, others will, too.

Amalia is a large woman with a sharp tongue. She is overbearing in her manner, speaks in clipped sentences, and is a poor listener. Amalia acts as though she has all the answers, no matter the subject. She does not disguise her disapproval of others; indeed she uses disapproval to keep others in check. She makes promises to get people off her back, then rarely follows up.

Amalia uses her job title to deflect criticism or feedback. She is simply not interested in what others think of her. Amalia is a bully. She believes that the best defense is a good offense. She further believes her strong personality commands respect and is the reason why no one challenges her authority.

Amalia would be shocked to learn that her colleagues do not take her seriously. They avoid interacting with her, no longer trust her to do what she says, and have stopped inviting her to meetings she used to be part of. Amalia has noticed this but shrugs it off, rationalizing that it gives her more time to pursue her objectives. She intends to play to a bigger and higher audience, mistakenly believing that this audience of superiors only sees what she shows them. Amalia is setting herself up for a fall.

The world today has become a lot like Missouri, the "show me" state. Talk is cheap. When your actions do not match your words, chances are you will be discounted as a person to put stock in. If you are inconsistent in word and deed over enough time, people who matter will ignore you. You say you'll meet Stan for lunch on Tuesday at noon and you show up at 12:10. Stan is mildly annoyed, but forgiving. Anyone can get caught on a phone call or stuck in traffic. Show up late three or four times for lunch with Stan and you're becoming untrustworthy. Make it a habit because Stan is always gracious and forgiving, now you're a flake.

Pay Attention

Several times a week, every week, I'll notice a woman walking with her head down, concentrating on her mobile device or chatting on a cell phone, making her way to wherever she is going, blissfully unaware of what is happening around her.

One morning, I watched a woman with a young child march out of a retail store and across a parking lot, never stopping to check for oncoming traffic or pay any attention whatsoever to the child behind her. But she wants to be taken seriously, just ask her!

The frequency and variety of these situations is on the rise, which heightens the danger for all of us. Just as we're often trying to accomplish too much which leads to endless schedule shuffling, we're often giving attention to things that just don't matter.

Do you really need to text your neighbor that you'll be home in ten minutes? Unless there is something in the oven or you are late picking up a child and her schedule is tight, that text is a throwaway.

Stop for a minute and think about your throwaway text messages, emails, phone calls and the like. How much time do you invest in these little nothings? How much of other people's time do you steal in making them read or listen to you?

How much of your day do you give to railing about injustices somewhere in the world? How about complaining to a co-worker about that witch with a 'b' in sales? Do you go on and on about gas prices? Food prices? Taxes? The weather? Your health? Your family's health? The stock market?

Do you take yourself seriously enough to value the way you invest your time and energy?

Several years ago, I sat next to a man on an airplane who was clearly agitated about something. He fidgeted constantly, clenched his armrests so hard his knuckles turned white, and pounded down a couple of straight vodkas. At first I was slightly amused, but the longer he carried on the more annoyed I grew. I ignored him as best I could until he slapped the open newspaper in front of him and said, "Look at this! This is terrible!"

I couldn't imagine what horrific scene he wanted to show me. When he pointed to a graph, I was confused. "What?" I said. He erupted with a loud dissertation about how the stock market is rigged, how he was getting screwed royally, how no matter how hard he worked, he would never regain what he was currently losing—couldn't I see how the line dropped off? The graph illustrated investment losses and it was ugly. My IRA took a hit along with everyone else's, so I understood his vexation.

Nodding sympathetically, I wondered out loud what he personally was going to do about it. That set off a second round of sputtering, which made me whisper a little prayer that he wouldn't have a heart attack before we landed. I continued to look at him in wonder until finally he started to laugh. 'You're right," he said. "Not a damn thing I can do." With that, he ordered another vodka shooter.

The point of that little story is that the world is full of things that make us angry. Some of them you can influence; many of them you can't. To risk your health and sanity railing against life's realities far beyond your reach is to lose the opportunity to make a difference where you are. It also means you are not paying attention to opportunities at hand. Scattering your energy so unproductively may make others reluctant to take you seriously when you really want them to.

My friend Nettie has a different problem. She is a gorgeous woman with a faithful husband and a son who loves to spend time with his dad playing racquetball. She is fortunate to be a stay-at-home mom and she volunteers several days a week at her son's school. Her biggest worries revolve around her son's attention and performance in school and her sore lower back.

Every once in a while, she and I commiserate on the cost of groceries or gas, but she admits she leaves the big worries to her husband. If a subject is not covered in People magazine, she is not likely to have an opinion on it. Most of the time, this suits her perfectly. No one comes to her seeking political debate or a deep discussion of world affairs. But sometimes she overhears someone talking about those things or the impact of a bit of legislation or the budgetary issues in town and she feels a little vulnerable because she doesn't know what they are talking about.

More important, when she ventures out beyond her circle of family and school friends, she does not feel as though people really 'see' her. They see her volunteer status or her role as wife and mother, but they don't seem to give her credit for having a brain. When we tick off the topics she feels confident talking about, she chuckles. No wonder.

The point here is not to wag a finger at women who do not have broad backgrounds, advanced education or sophisticated interests, but to say that if you want to be admitted into different circles or have others take you seriously beyond a certain image you portray, you would be wise to pay attention to a broader picture of life. Exploring the world and all its gifts and mysteries is a wonderful way to add energy to your life and put a sparkle in your eye. Believe me, people will notice.

Manage Your Maladies

Ladies, please, if you want to be taken seriously, stop talking about what hurts. This includes physical aches and pains, chronic health situations, and the emotional pain caused by uncaring partners, wayward children, or insensitive bosses.

Life dumps on everyone at one time or another and you can bet that while you're focused on your pain, someone else is enduring something at least as difficult. I am reminded of the old saying, "If we all threw our problems in a pile and saw everyone else's, we'd grab ours back."

Why do some people (especially women) feel the need to talk endlessly about their struggles? I can't answer that except to say that maybe it is the way they have learned to get attention. Maybe they believe that by making their challenges known, they will be shown greater kindness or compassion. Maybe they have simply developed a bad habit.

Here is the truth. No one wants to listen to a litany of woe. Not from a friend or a partner, neighbor, or spouse.

There are specific maladies women discuss that destroy their credibility as serious people faster than ice cream melts on a hot summer day. The biggest no-no is anything related to 'female' health. Discussion of personal gynecological issues, menopausal issues, even breast cancer makes other people uncomfortable. It's gross.

Let's make a distinction. Talking about these issues in a general sense—tracking trends, discussing healthcare developments and their impact on the workforce, society, or specific regions of the world—is much different than voicing your personal struggles. While women's health is of significant interest to many, your maladies are not.

There is a scenario so common it has become a classic example of how not to be taken seriously. Two women are chatting at the grocery checkout line. One is the cashier, the other bags the groceries. One says, "I have had this pain 'down there' for weeks. I'm starting to get worried about it. Her co-worker replies, "I know what you mean. And it's especially bad when I sleep with my boyfriend." No!

> *Reality is the leading cause of stress among those in touch with it.*
> - Lily Tomlin

Not only is this casual chatter painfully inappropriate, it tells anyone who happens to overhear it that these two are dumb and dumber. They are oblivious to who might overhear them or how they might encounter these people later. One woman I know left a job at a retail pharmacy and began looking for work elsewhere. During her time at the pharmacy, she developed the bad habit of complaining about her sore wrists and bad back. Another woman who happened to hear this was a human resources executive who knew a lot of people. When she learned that the woman was looking for a new job, she warned her friends that this woman was a chronic complainer in ill health.

Yes, we live in a tell-all world where people say the craziest things. You may believe that sharing personal information is a way to bond with others or signal your desire to become friends. If you want to be taken seriously, don't do it.

The same is true for relationship issues. Heartbreak over lost love is a topic as old as time. How you feel about the jerk that led you on then dumped you is of no interest to anyone outside your small circle of friends and family. This is another common topic among retail co-workers, especially when customer traffic is light. Don't go there.

Ditto for complaints about your slug of a husband who does not finish projects he starts, does not open doors for you any-more, or who belches in company. We all deal with a host of irritants day in and day out. We don't want to hear about yours.

If you want help, ask. Most people are willing to share what they have learned. If you are looking for attention, a smarter way to get it is to accomplish something, then offer to share what you have learned.

Here's a tip: high maintenance equals low credibility. Divas are out, even in Hollywood. They were never in anywhere else. Insist on special attention and treatment and you'll guarantee your place on a list of people not to be taken seriously. Ever. For any reason.

Same for hypochondriacs. They are psychological leeches because they are never satisfied with feeling well, always certain that even on pain free days something sinister is brewing inside, and they have an incessant need to tell you about it. You know how long you stay interested in their story. That's about how long someone is interested in yours.

People who talk too much, who are constantly asking questions or demanding attention, who cavalierly order others around or insist on being served in particular ways, are examples of high-maintenance people. They have low credibility and next to zero chance of being taken seriously.

Life throws a lot of stuff at you: A wrinkled skirt, broken fingernail, bad haircut, spoiled food, spilled coffee, disloyal friend, cheating partner. These and a million other maladies are part of an active life. We feel for you, sister, and trust you to manage them. Please don't disappoint us.

CHAPTER FIVE
LET THEM BE

As I have mentioned several times in this book, women are socialized and expected to be caretakers. I sincerely hope this never changes. However, as a life-long champion of people everywhere and from all walks of life to discover, develop and utilize their special talents, the notion of giving oneself entirely to the care and development of others, often at your own expense, never made sense to me. Notice two important words: *entirely* and *expense*.

As a caregiver, whether by nature or by virtue of your role in caring for a child, partner, parent or other loved one, your investment in another is precious. Any time your love and

attention gives comfort, instruction, assurance, and peace to another, you do beautiful and meaningful work. But sacrificing yourself in the process is unnecessary and dumb. Forgive my bluntness in this, but it is true.

My favorite Irish shrink has counseled me on this in recent years. I am a helper, like most women I know. Our tendency is to give time to others when we don't really have it. The demands and deadlines of our lives are real! Yet our tendency to respond to need regardless of what is happening in our world not only enables others in their needy ways, it creates an expectation that when they reach out, we will respond if not immediately, then quickly. On the rare occasion that we don't, we are susceptible to criticism that our response was too slow.

Which brings me to *expense*. Think about what we have discussed in this book so far. The idea that your beauty is unique, so of special value. That substance is developed through challenge. That the roles you play are varied and they change with life's chapters. That the presence you create and the seriousness with which others consider you are of your making. And now we look at what is your responsibility and what is not. When you invest in someone else's wellbeing or success at the expense of your own, you throw away much of what this book is suggesting. That's yours to do, of course. You are free to make your life the way you want it to be. In fact, you're the only one who can.

If you want your life to be one of complete service to whoever needs it no matter the circumstances, you can skip this chapter. If, however, you want to support and help others while creating a life of richness and meaning for yourself, please keep reading.

The Beatles smash hit Let It Be was released as a single in March 1970 and became the title of their twelfth and final studio album in May that year. Echoing those words of wisdom, sometimes the wisest form of help is to let others be. Leave them alone. Send them to their rooms to think about what they have done and what they want to do next.

You Can't Change Others

One of the most difficult truths to get into your mind, heart, and psyche is the fact that you simply cannot change another human being. No, you can't! No matter how much you love someone, agonize over their mistakes and pain, or have the perfect solution to their problem, your best advice and support will be of no use if they are not interested or ready to behave differently. Think back to the things about yourself others thought you should change. A bad habit. Your choice of food or drink. Your selection of friends, hobbies, or clothing.

Your reaction to their advice was probably negative for the most part; maybe at best neutral on good days. Yet, the other person who may have claimed to know you better than you know yourself only meant to help you be a better person. Why, then, did you so vigorously reject their suggestion?

> *We cannot change anything until we accept it. Condemnation does not liberate, it oppresses.*
> - Carl Jung

Very simply, most of us feel as though we are doing the best we can. Given other circumstances—a different childhood or an over-flowing bank account—yes, we might be different. But we don't have those other things. So we have adapted and become who we are, thank you very much. That's how other people feel about your well-meaning suggestions.

Early in a relationship be it friendship, a working relationship, or a love affair, you probably view the shortcomings of your partner as charming quirks. Over time these may become irritants. With enough exposure, you may decide they are character flaws that need to be fixed. This is when you begin to offer advice or nag or bully others into doing what you want them to do. It never works.

Neil Diamond and Barbara Streisand sang a duet, "You Don't Bring Me Flowers Anymore." The song mourns what used to be and by implication could be again if only you who once brought flowers would be willing to change back to the way you were. It captures the sadness that many feel when people they love won't be who they used to be and maybe never were. You can't change people. What you can change is what you are telling yourself about them that makes you unhappy.

The *Wall Street Journal* ran a special section on New Year's Resolutions at the end of 2011. One of the brilliant ideas was to let other people make your resolutions for you. We all have blind spots, the article claimed, so others can be helpful in pointing out areas of weakness for us to fix. I laughed as I read it. The assumption underlying this helpful suggestion seemed to be that people who care about you know better than you do what you need to work on. For what purpose, I wondered? To what end? Talk about an open invitation to busybodies!

Family members could be especially helpful, I suppose, because they feel entitled by virtue of birth to be brutally honest. For your good of course. Because they love you. What could possibly go wrong?

Sarcasm aside, ideas such as these are well intended, of course. But the opportunity for unintended consequences is enormous. Offering feedback when invited is one thing. Suggesting improvements to help someone be a better person is an invitation to argument. Yes, there are people in relationships who do want others to tell them what they should change in order to make for more perfect unions. Wonderful. That's a different proposition from listening to someone's litany of your imperfections, no matter how well-meaning. You don't appreciate their help in changing you. Guess what. They don't appreciate yours, either.

As a woman of beauty and substance you know that everyone has dreams and demons that are sometimes best worked out in private. Unless you are asked directly for help or advice, let them be.

Their Viewpoint is Valid

Here is an important thing to remember: Every person you come into contact with from your immediate family to friends and co-workers to strangers on the street, in stores, and at school, has grown up differently than you did.

They see the world differently. They experienced different events, felt different emotions, and reacted to things based on what they knew or needed to learn. Their viewpoint is every bit as

valid as yours, even though it may be very different. Given this truth, it's a wonder so many people learn to get along!

Not one human being sees life in exactly the same way as another. No one wants exactly the same things. No one likes exactly the same things. We get hungry at different times, scared by different things, excited by different ideas, and angry at still different triggers. Yet, we all want to be understood.

The adage, "Seek first to understand, then to be understood" is grand advice. Yet it is very difficult to quiet your own desire to be understood in order to try to understand someone else. It doesn't happen on its own; you have to consciously decide to set aside your need if you are to have a chance at understanding another. That's tough to do.

In my workshops, I will often introduce this notion to help people relax their grip on things they know to be absolutely true. To illustrate, I will ask someone in the audience to put their hands on either side of their face creating blinders, then look straight ahead and describe the room in detail. I then ask someone in a different section of the room to do the same. Their descriptions rarely match. One sees a bank of windows; the other sees a doorway or a wall hung with mirrors or artwork.

To round out the exercise and make my point, I then describe what I see, insisting that my view of the room must be correct since I am leading the workshop! I invite the other two to challenge my description. On occasion, a brave soul does. More often, however, the others fall silent with doubtful looks on their faces. They judge their viewpoint less valid than mine because they are there to learn and I am there to teach. How unfortunate!

Being a lover of football, I use a penalty flag as another example. When my team—the Green Bay Packers—is penalized, I'll often jump off the couch, shouting, "No way! You're nuts!"

referring of course to the referee. My cat, thrown from my lap, settles in nearby. The dog bolts from the room.

As the play is shown from across the field on a replay camera—a completely opposite perspective—I sometimes have to concede the penalty. My view, though very clear, was limited. As a result of my absolutely certain knowledge being disproved, I've learned to sit down, shut up and endure the good-natured abuse I sometimes get.

Here's the point: We all sit in a different seat in the arena of life. Where we were born, how we were raised, the experiences we had growing up, the good or bad luck, the helpful or hurtful people we encountered along life's pathway, make each one of us different. Unique. A gem. That includes you. And the rest of us benefit when you can describe what you see.

Over lunch with Rick and Marcy one day, our conversation wandered onto this subject of whose viewpoint is valid. Which tells me that it is on people's minds and in their hearts, whether they are willing to admit it or not.

Rick volunteered that Marcy finds fault with a lot of things he does for her, even though he can't understand why she gets irritated. Marcy says Rick doesn't listen to her; that the things he does please him, not her. He countered by saying he wished she would just believe that he loves her. Leaning over, he gave her a hug.

Marcy wrinkled her nose, furrowed her brow, and grunted.

And then the fight began.

Both Rick and Marcy have pictures in their minds of what a spouse should do to contribute to a happy marriage. Never mind that they have not shared these mental images with each other. Marcy believes that if you love someone, you should know, somehow, what the other person wants or needs. Rick believes that if you paid attention to actions, you would know you are loved. Houston, we have a problem.

The field of education is roiling with debate over what to teach, how to teach, how to measure what you teach, and what to do with kids who can't seem to learn. Having spent time working with New York City public schools as well as several charter schools in Texas, I am struck by the passion and stiff-necked stubbornness of people who disagree with one another while insisting they have the right answer. Right answers seem to be more important than effective solutions during a lot of these discussions. If you listen past the fear that emerges, you can hear perfectly valid points from almost everyone.

> *When we are no longer able to change a situation, we are challenged to change ourselves.*
> - Victor E. Frankl

The trouble is that people have blinders on and are seeing only what is in front of them. They point to it with great vigor, demanding others to see what is in plain sight! Naturally, everyone else with blinders on is doing the same from different perspectives. The noise becomes deafening and no one is willing either to drop their blinders or move over to see what someone else sees. That's funny when you think about it. Say you were the brave soul who walked over to check out someone else's blinkered reality. You wouldn't lose the knowledge you have; you know what you've seen with your own eyes after all. But maybe, just maybe if you saw what that other person sees so clearly, your understanding of the bigger issue might be deepened. Your perspective might be shifted ever so slightly.

But nobody wants to admit that his or her vision is limited and heaven forbid anyone admit to being wrong! Ironically, these passionate debates center on what's good for the kids even though we rarely talk to them.

When someone wants to argue with you insisting that you are dead wrong and they are absolutely right, don't try to match shout for shout, tit for tat, or "fact" for "fact." Acknowledge that, in their view, they are correct. Of course, you know you are correct in yours. If you wish to seek common ground in order to strengthen your relationship, please seek it. But don't waste time insisting that someone see your point of view in exactly the way you wish it to be seen. Their viewpoint is valid, too.

Their Messes Are Not Your Problem

You've heard the expression, "A woman's work is never done." It's true. There is always something to clean, fold, put away, shop for, take out, design, deliver, or fix to keep us busy for ten lifetimes. And that's without cleaning up the messes other people make.

It can be very difficult to learn that someone you care about is in trouble. But it happens. Your first thought might be to wonder how you can help. Can you love them enough or cook well enough or joke them out of their issue? Let the thought pass. Their mess is not your problem.

Several years ago a friend who had shopped her way to financial disaster approached me. Thinking that I was financially set and begging for confidentiality, she asked me for help to the tune of $5,000.

My answer was swift and easy to share: No. Not only did I not have that kind of money stashed somewhere, I had no stake in the problem she had created for herself.

Her disappointment and near panic about what to do next caused her to say some very hurtful things using language that would make a sailor blush. (Apologies to gentlemanly sailors.)

She accused me of being a lousy effing friend, someone who was not as effing nice as I wanted people to think, even effing un-Christian in my unwillingness to help her. Naturally, she was not in the least bit interested in understanding the source of the problem, which was her practice of shopping for new clothes, shoes, jewelry and household furnishings any time she felt bored or unhappy or just needed a little boost. Similarly, she was not interested in learning how to create a budget for herself.

Frankly, I could sympathize. My skill with numbers and patience with the budgeting process is sorely limited. But I am blessed with an innate practicality and my survival instincts have kept me living within my means. I am no better a person than she, but my weaknesses have not landed me in financial hot water.

Ultimately, we ended the friendship. I could not, indeed would not, accept responsibility for helping her clean up a big mess. She had not sought my advice or help as she was spending her way into trouble, so expecting me to shoulder the burden for resolving the situation was, in my mind, illogical, disrespectful and frankly a requirement of friendship that I was not interested in meeting. Especially without consultation up front.

It hurt to lose the friendship. I was stung by her nasty words and accusations of being mean and uncaring. I was shocked to listen to a woman I considered a friend revile me in the crudest of terms. For a few seconds, I even worried about what she might say to others to turn them against me. There was a time in my life when I would have responded to these feelings of hurt and worry and done whatever I could to help her. I am a helper, after all.

But I knew her accusations were not true. I understood her fear and desperation to get out of a scary situation. I simply did not have a responsibility to make things right for her. So I let her be, with a prayer that she find her way out of her financial hole and in the process learn to put some restraints on her spending.

This was difficult! I could have given in; there were moments when I thought it would be the easier, kinder, and nobler decision. I could have talked with some people I knew who might have been more immediately helpful to her. I could have given her some money. In doing these things, I could have patted myself on the back as the kind of person who would do anything for a friend.

I cringed at things I did not want to hear from her; words that struck at my sense of self. "You've changed. You used to care about people. I thought you were my friend." Manipulative statements, of course. But effective in that they made me feel awful and almost second-guess my decision.

Had I accepted responsibility for assisting however I could, I would not have truly helped her. I would have, instead, provided an escape hatch from her troubles. I would have taught her on some level that no matter how badly she behaved, she could turn to friends who would rescue her. I would have helped her stay in trouble.

My daughters may or may not remember a particular conversation we had before they went off to college, but in it I told them three things:

1) If you get yourself into trouble, find a way to get yourself out of it.

2) If you need my help, tell me only what I need to know in order to help you.

3) I will look forward to hearing the rest of the story sometime after you graduate. Maybe decades after you graduate.

What was unstated in this advice, but central in my thoughts, was that I trusted them to explore a bigger world than they knew growing up in our home. Indeed, I was excited about it! I fully expected that they would make mistakes and I trusted their ability to think things through and find a solution. Did I expect this process to be easy or comfortable? No. But I was not interested in their comfort or ease. I was interested in their learning. I wanted them to discover their capacity for solving problems and for digging their way out of holes they dug for themselves. I also remembered my own embarrassing adventures as a young adult and would never have wanted my mother to know some of the details! I still don't. And she doesn't. Holding one's tongue is a subject for another book.

The most important lesson in all this is that if I had swooped in to save them, they would never have learned how strong, smart, and clever they are. If I had tried to fix their every problem, they may have learned to trust me, but they would not have had the opportunity to learn to trust themselves.

Another type of mess that is irresistible to women happens when people treat each other badly. Or appear to.

Kari was clearly distressed when she told me about an exchange she overheard between two people in her office. One was a supervisor, who spoke in a very condescending manner to his direct report. She argued that their nasty words and tone of voice created a hostile working environment. No supervisor should be allowed to talk that way to a subordinate. In her indignation, Kari wanted to intervene somehow, to set a higher standard for the two of them. She was quite beside herself about the situation.

I asked if the subordinate complained about the way the supervisor treated her. No. Did the subordinate show ill effects from the exchange like a sullen attitude or drop off in performance? No. Did other people in the office complain about the way they worked together? No. Could it be that the supervisor and subordinate had worked out a way of arguing that worked for them? That what sounded like anger or derision was nothing more than the way they challenge one another?

So no one else was bothered by the spirited discussion, least of all the subordinate whose feelings Kari felt compelled to protect. Turns out it was a mess that didn't need her clean-up skills.

Every day in a million ways people create messes. You don't need to be arbiter or janitor. Learn to be okay with stepping around them, or noticing and calling in other help. "Clean up in Aisle 8."

It's Not Personal

It can be very difficult to accept that when things go wrong or unfold in ways you didn't expect, that it is not because of something you said or did or because of the kind of person you are. This is especially true with regard to relationships.

Women have an automatic reaction to this that I swear is genetic. When something goes wrong in a meeting, a conversation, a friendship, an online date, or heaven knows what else, our first thought is, "What did I do?" Meaning what did I do to cause a conversation to go wrong, a friendship to derail or a love interest to head for the hills? This is the cause of an incredible amount of unnecessary suffering and more often than not, it is not about you. Please read that again. It is not about you!

Don Miguel Ruiz in his best-selling book, *The Four Agreements*, presents this as the second of four agreements. *Don't take anything personally*. He says that nothing others do is because of you. What others say and do is a projection of their own reality, their own dream.

That's big. I'm not sure it's that black and white—'nothing' is akin to 'always' and 'never' in my mind—but the point is that you will waste a lot of time and energy and experience heartache beyond belief if you insist on making things personal.

I will admit it took me a long time to get this and begin to live it. For a long time, I was sure that certain unhappy situations and relationships were absolutely because of me—specifically some defect in me—that caused them to get messed up or end when I wanted more than anything for them to be part of my life forever.

When I began to see that others live in their worlds as I live in mine—that they understand their surroundings based on how they grew up, what they have experienced, and what they have learned to embrace or protect themselves from—I started to realize that some shadows from our experiences cloud our lives to this day. We don't always see others as they are. Our actions are not always based on what is happening now, but what may have happened at other times.

Without getting too shrinky about all this, suffice to say that you will be stronger, happier, and saner when you accept that others being themselves will sometimes create separation from you. Conversely, sometimes you being you will cause others to want to be somewhere else. It's not because we are deficient, as I used to think, it's because we are different.

Leaving others alone is not a personal dismissal; it is a practical means of protecting your time and energy and allowing others to work through their stuff. This can be an extraordinary gift of respect if understood properly. Granted, it can be difficult to explain, especially if someone you want to leave alone is hurting or wanting more than anything to be with you.

In the same way, when people choose not to spend time with you, it is not necessarily because they are rejecting you. Perhaps they, too, have decided on certain priorities to which they are dedicating their time, attention, and energy.

Should you have the misfortune of enduring a friend or family member's disappointment or anger, pause a moment to consider the circumstances. Your friend may be having a hard time with life. Harsh words may reflect inner pain or struggle that has nothing to do with you. Criticism may be unfair, even unjust. The story being told may bear no resemblance to reality. Don't try to correct it in the moment. Even though words are coming directly at you, do not make them about you. Do not take them personally.

Additionally, you would be wise to not decide the future of your friendship based on this current situation. We all encounter dips, even sink holes, in life. Surely you would not want your friends to ditch you because you behaved badly at a low point in your life. Surely you will not cast aside a friend or relative because she is behaving like the wicked witch. Will you?

And now a reality check. You may be thinking to yourself, "Really? Am I a saint? Who is doing this for me?"

You may also be thinking that every once in a while it is personal. That 'perfect' friend who always gets what she wants and never has to struggle has finally encountered something that takes her down a notch or two. Good! She needs to feel what the rest of us feel once in a while! While these private feelings are natural and seem to come most often when we are tired or discouraged, they do not represent you at your strongest, finest hour. Women of beauty and substance deal with the grungy realities of life, including feelings that are less than charitable. But they don't beat themselves up over them. They don't allow others to, either.

> *Pride makes us artificial and humility makes us real.*
> - Thomas Merton

Promising yourself to take nothing personal is a wonderful way to stay engaged with people and life, even when neither seems very attractive.

One final word before we leave this chapter. In no way am I advocating a washing-of-hands approach to things that are legitimately your responsibility. If you have a hand in creating dysfunction, you have a responsibility to try to clear things up.

For example, as a parent it is not enough to throw your kid out into the world, expecting that by trial and error he will figure out right from wrong, good from evil, or worthwhile from wasteful. Your job is to instruct, guide, and correct as many times as it takes for them to understand. Family activities, church attendance, the schools you send them to, and any community involvement you may engage in all play a role in shaping their values. Additionally, how you behave demonstrates what you believe to be right. And believe me, they are watching!

In the same way, if you hire a new employee, your first order of responsibility is to explain to that person what the business is about, how their job fits into the overall operation of the company, what the rules of engagement are, and other particulars regarding employment. Explaining aside, you show them how things really work by the decisions you make, the things you pay attention to and those you ignore, and how you interact with others inside and outside the company.

It is within this framework that you decide when to let someone be. As mentioned earlier, the messes of the people around you are not yours to clean up unless you have had a hand in making them.

CHAPTER SIX

EMBRACING RISK

A nd now we come to a subject that makes a lot of people nervous. Risk. It is the third element of Backbone: Intelligent, purposeful risk taking. It follows competence and confidence. As a result it is not reckless or mindless. Still, no matter how many times I said those qualifying words when I first began to talk about Backbone, people tensed up. At a meeting of start-up gurus, I was told flat out to quit using the word risk.

"Why?" I asked.

"It scares people," was the reply.

Which pretty much made my point. We scare ourselves with the silliest things sometimes. A little word shuts people down? Yes, of course. I know. Words are powerful. People are sensitive.

The only way to have a life that is interesting, meaningful and fun is to go create it. That's right. You can't dream or wish or imagine it into being, you have to literally go make it. Many years ago, when my daughters were little, I printed a bumper sticker of sorts and taped it to my refrigerator. "No Guts, No Story" it said in bold, black letters.

> Only those who will risk going too far can possibly find out how far one can go.
> - T.S. Eliot

The girls scoffed at me. "Mom, can't you get anything right? It's 'No Guts, No Glory'!" I smiled at their youthful disdain and explained. "Glory comes and goes. When your life is over it is going to tell a story. If you never do anything, the story will be quick to tell and probably pretty boring. But if you try things and touch people and learn as much as you can, your story is going to be interesting, maybe informative and who knows, it might inspire somebody else to create a neat story, too!"

Risk has earned a bad reputation as a dirty word, associated as it often is with situations that have high upside/high downside potential. Investment decisions, extreme sports stunts, even some marriage proposals are examples of risky situations.

We don't like to consider our world in terms of risk, but it is all around us. Think about it. When you turn off your alarm and roll out of bed, there is a risk of turning your ankle and losing your balance. You could fall and break something.

On your way to work, some goofball could be texting instead of paying attention to traffic. His swerving could nick the corner of another bumper, causing the car to spin out in front of you. You can't stop, so you plow into this car, totally destroying yours.

Your child's cough could be a product of hanging around sick kids at daycare or it could signal a life-threatening illness. Your decision to wait and see if it gets worse could be the right one or the very wrong one.

Saying the wrong thing at the wrong time can deep-six job opportunities, derail friendships and brand you undesirable. Risk is all around us. What to do?

Embrace it.

Elizabeth struggled with her weight for many years. After a shocking and unexpected divorce, she packed on more pounds, eating to assuage her devastated feelings. Desperate for help, she read books on dieting, took classes in nutrition, and joined several different gyms, but she could not get her weight under control.

Finally she decided on bariatric surgery. She researched the risks before, during, and after the procedure. They were substantial. Knowing what she was up against, Elizabeth sought support from friends and family and chose a well-respected surgeon. The procedure was successful and Elizabeth gradually and systematically revised the way she lives and eats. Risk can be your friend if you are willing to see it clearly and choose an appropriate response to it.

Your Appetite

One key to successfully embracing risk is to first understand your appetite for it. The word risk means very different things to people. Some people consider asking a question with the boss in the room to be high risk. Some people consider sky diving as risky. Truth is, there are risks that scare you and others that don't. Usually the ones that don't scare you are similar to things you have already learned or experienced in some way. You no longer consider them risks.

Over the years, you have constructed a comfort zone made up of millions of interactions with life. Chances are good you repeated things that felt good and vowed to avoid things that felt bad. Whether these interactions involved food, travel, people, language, play, work or study, they formed your preferences and ultimately your appetite for risk.

Watch young children at play for a simple but clear illustration of this. Lilly loves to sing and dance and doesn't hesitate to take the stage at the children's museum to enact her own variety show. Her cousin, Maya, also a ham at home, shrinks from the public stage. Yet, when Maya takes Lilly's hand to ride a roller coaster together, Lilly shakes her off and escapes to the safety of her mother's side. Different risks; different reactions.

Grown-ups are no different. Some people see risk in expressing a contrary point of view. Some consider trying a new restaurant risky. Certainly starting a business, moving across the country for a new job, or leaving a long-term relationship involve risk. For many women, saying 'no' is loaded with risk.

The point is your appetite for risk is unique to you. Learning its boundaries and depth is a great place to begin expansion, if that is what you wish to do. If you have decided you are pretty much done growing, that's okay, too. Just recognize this decision and accept the risk that comes with atrophy. Recognize, too, that growth around you will likely make you uncomfortable.

Debra wants to take a scuba diving course and she wants her friend Carrie to take it with her. Debra grew up near water and is very comfortable being in it. She took swimming lessons as a child, served as a lifeguard in high school, and has vacationed at water-themed resorts many times. Her friend, Carrie, grew up in a big city. She never took swimming lessons, has not spent any time to speak of near water and, although she is intrigued by the idea of learning to scuba dive, she is scared to death to try it.

Remember our discussion about different points of view being valid? The same is true for different appetites for risk. You don't need to defend yours, just know what it is.

My friend Rachel loves to take risk for the adrenaline rush it provides. She was one of the first to bungee jump when the craze hit the U.S. in the 1980s. She has traveled to exotic places, cooked inventive meals, and revels in being the most provocative person in the room. Naturally, she is admired by some and reviled by others. It's all the same to her.

Kim, on the other hand, has a strong aversion to risk. Just shy of obsessive-compulsive, she checks and double-checks her actions each day. Kim is an expert in physical safety, technological precaution, and proper behavior at home, school, work, church, and community. Her friends say she can be very funny sometimes, but mostly she is an enigma. Kim is careful not to reveal much about herself.

As you might imagine, talking about risk with Diane is fun. Talking about risk with Kim, not so much. As you might also imagine, Diane's life is more interesting to others than Kim's, however Kim finds many ways to stay interested in the world around her. It's just that her exploration is more private and circumspect. Both women have discovered their personal appetite for risk.

Enablers and Barriers

While the notion of constructing a comfort zone may be new to you, be assured you have been an active agent. The fact that you are reading this book is testimony to your curiosity and interest in making life good and meaningful. You have made many decisions so far and the result of those decisions has placed you right where you are. Like cartoon character Ziggy on a map marked by a red X, "You are here" because of choices you have made over time.

Some of those choices were made because of barriers you encountered. The Glass Ceiling is a classic one we explored in Chapter Three. Discrimination is another giant historical barrier many women have faced. Role expectations, physical limitations, even family of origin can create barriers that are real. The disapproval of others and fear of the unknown are barriers that spring up in your mind and can be the worst of all. Because they are private and invisible, no one knows about them.

When you stop yourself from doing things that others believe would be easy for you, they naturally wonder. Sometimes they ask and sometimes they just raise an eyebrow. That raised eyebrow represents the risk of disapproval. It is something a lot of women will do just about anything to avoid.

Julie longed to join the military. Her boyfriend was a US Marine serving in Afghanistan; her family boasted a long line of military servicemen from her great-grandfather through every generation until hers. Her two brothers chose other careers, much to the disappointment of her father.

But when Julie said she was going to join the Marines, her family was aghast. Why? No other woman in the family had ever served; it wasn't quite right. They didn't want to think of Julie being in harm's way. After all, she was going to be a mother one day, wasn't she?

While Julie struggled through the rigors of boot camp, an aunt took to gossiping about her real intentions. She wondered aloud about Julie's perceived need for attention, her unusual career choice and went so far as to question her sexual orientation. No family member had ever behaved quite so strangely.

On the day Julie was sworn in as a US Marine, her family was suddenly so very proud. With Julie's achievement they could now boast four generations of unbroken military service. Aren't they something? Aren't they special? What a wonderful family!

Nobody mentioned the bad aunt's gossip. Nobody remembered the way they questioned Julie's decision. All they knew was how proud they were of this amazing family. Was Julie angry with this remarkable about face? No. She didn't become a Marine for them. As a woman of tremendous beauty and substance, she did it for her own reasons. And she really didn't care if the family wanted to take credit.

While life's barriers may or may not be tangible, they do serve to slow you down. Finding ways around, under, over or through barriers can take a lot of time and energy. It's worth the effort when you know where you're going.

Enablers are those people, places and things that help move you forward despite the presence of risk. They may be as coincidental as a series of green lights on your way out of town or as intentional as business relationships you work hard to develop.

Your enablers may include education, good health—physical and spiritual—financial resources, a strong community, and a healthy network. Good weather, plentiful resources and a resilient spirit are enablers, too. In short, anything that supports you in stepping outside your comfort zone to embrace risk is an enabler.

Tina is an aggressive young professional who takes pride in her intelligence, energy and ability to crank out a lot of work. She writes marketing proposals that are both strategic and detailed in half the time it takes her colleagues. She expects to be rewarded for her talent and has successfully negotiated substantial raises during her company's annual review process.

Tina had a close and friendly working relationship with her boss, who appreciated her productivity and respected her ability. He recognized that her style could be abrasive at times and privately counseled her to 'take it easy.' When predictable jealousy cropped up among Tina's peers, he made little jokes about Tina's drive and persistence, hoping to demonstrate that he was not going to defend her but he wasn't going to criticize her either. After all, she was a star who brought in big business for the department. Tina's boss was an enabler in the sense that he challenged and supported her, gave her visibility with clients, and helped build her career.

All was well until Tina got promoted. Suddenly her peers were one notch below her and the green-eyed monster of jealousy broke free. You can imagine the stories that began circulating about her relationship with the boss. Despite clear evidence of professional competence and extraordinary success with clients, former peers concocted the ugly cliché that Tina had slept her way to the top. The boss, once considered a champion and enabler, now because of gossip and rivalry among his other direct reports, became a barrier to her professional status within the company. In time, Tina quit.

This tale of bad behavior among co-workers is a familiar one and women are especially vulnerable. You may argue with Tina's ultimate decision, but it turned out to be the wisest choice for her. Was it a risk? Sure. But staying would have been, too.

She had learned as much as she could learn and reached the top of her earning capability at the company. Her relationship with colleagues, though never close or particularly warm, had turned toxic. While her decision to leave was not easy or comfortable, she decided to leverage her boss's goodwill in the form of a glowing reference letter, which landed her a great new job in a bigger firm. The barrier once again became an enabler.

Once we believe in ourselves, we can risk curiosity, wonder, spontaneous delight, or any experience that reveals the human spirit.

- e.e. cummings

This story is relatively easy to tell; it was a hellish time for everyone concerned. It is important to recognize that sometimes enablers—including your own talent and drive—can be misconstrued and turned against you. When this happens, you have a choice: to focus on the barrier or find a way to leverage an asset.

Your world holds a host of both enablers and barriers to the things you want to do. Perhaps the greatest enabler or barrier of all resides within your cranium. Your mind can talk you into or out of anything you wish! I have been fighting my own mental chatter as I was writing this book. "What did you write that for? It sounds dumb. What if nobody understands your point? What if nobody agrees with you?"

These noisy thoughts are dandelions in your mental landscape. Though you do not plant them, they burst forth and multiply. Though you may try to eradicate them, they are stubborn in their refusal to go away—and stay away! Navigating your barriers and leveraging your enablers requires awareness, careful consideration and the courage to act. Every choice carries its share of risk.

Some Realities

To effectively embrace risk, you need to be clear-eyed about reality. Yes, I know the word reality can be every bit as scary to people as the word risk. Indeed, some people go to mighty extremes to avoid seeing the world as it is. They have too much invested in making the world what they need it to be. I'm convinced this inability to see and deal with reality is the biggest cause of destructive behaviors. It is certainly a major cause of the fear I encounter in working with people.

In the spirit of developing ever-deeper beauty and substance, let's take a look at some realities. For starters, you may have noticed that the world is ordered according to power and influence. I am not talking here about political parties or any particular ideology, but rather that certain people and groups have the ability to make things happen. Think of your school, company, community, social group or family. Someone calls the shots. If you don't like the shots that are called and think you can do better, you are free to work on gaining a position of power. That's reality. You may try and fail. You may obtain decision-making authority and call shots other people don't like. It's all reality, which is what makes life so interesting.

Studies have consistently shown that attractive people get the best jobs, quickest promotions and most-coveted awards. Seems we like to talk with, buy from and hang around with people who are pleasing to the eye.

As the story of Tina pointed out, however, attractive people are often targets of the meanest gossip, most vicious personal attacks, and outright lies. You may be thinking that a good job, tons of money, and lots of friends and supporters would help you deal with gossip, if only you had the chance to prove it. That's how grass-is-always-greener people think.

Your physical beauty will fade. There are many procedures to help you stall the aging process, but time leaves its mark on us all. The great news about time, however, is that it allows you to deepen your knowledge and develop a rich and unique beauty. You have one lifetime to shape the most amazing you. Get busy.

You will make mistakes. Probably many. You may be hurt by some of your mistakes. But if you continue to focus on who you are becoming, you will find that mistakes can be wonderful instructors.

This truth about mistakes as instructors is a difficult one to accept. If you are like most people, you know intellectually that you will make mistakes, but you want to believe that the ones you make will be little ones, private ones, barely noticeable by others. Oh, if only that were true! When you make an epic mistake—and we all do at one time or another—your embarrassment and sometimes sheer mortification at the ugliness of it can cripple you. Remember Barbara, our black sheep friend from Chapter One? She made a bunch of really big really bad mistakes and she overcame each one.

Here's another challenging reality. We trust experts when we are keen to do the right thing and we are uncertain of what that is. In reality, experts will never know you as well as you know yourself. And they cannot know what your heart desires.

I remember vividly wanting to take the right courses as I began my college career. I wanted to be a journalist. And I wanted to avoid algebra! It's funny now to remember this, but my fear of algebra, tied to an embarrassing grade as a high school freshman crippled my effectiveness.

A high school counselor laid out my list of required courses for the first two years of college. On it: a five-credit zoology lab course and college algebra. Why do I remember these courses but cannot recall most of the others? They were both dreadful experiences. I was afraid of making mistakes and this fear guaranteed my poor performance.

I was intimidated by the zoology professor who told the class during our first meeting that he was fonder of animals than people and that he preferred his animals dead. I thought he was joking. As I observed him over the course of that class, it became clear he was not. Though I was fascinated by the subject matter and managed to overcome my queasiness during dissections, my confidence throughout the class was very low. As a result my performance was not what I expected of myself. My fear of being judged deficient by a professor I did not like or respect amounted to a huge waste of energy.

This is one small example of how we become distracted by fear. Maybe there is someone in your life who makes you nervous because you think this person is watching and waiting for you to make a mistake. There may be. And this person may use your mistake to try to make you feel foolish or deficient. It happens. But you do not have to participate! When you can embrace the risk that you will make mistakes, you can accept your goofs and keep moving forward.

Here's another reality. You will encounter people who want to compete with you for life's goodies. People who compete often have a need to be the best and believe that life's gifts are limited. They must get theirs before you get yours. Acknowledge this reality. Do not spend time with these people. They will seek to diminish your ideas and accomplishments in order to advance their own.

And one final reality. When you attempt to do something out of the ordinary—and in this case growing on purpose is out of the ordinary—some people will want to shut you down using words.

Simple words like "selfish" and "judgmental" are intended to make you feel self-conscious and bad. Selfish means you are too concerned with your own wellbeing; you demonstrate a lack of regard for others. But there are lots of self- words. We know, for example, that there is a big difference between self-absorbed and self-aware, between self-centered and self-assured.

A self-absorbed woman has a very small frame of reference. Indeed, it starts inside her mind and extends about as far as her reach. She judges everything around her by the way it impacts her. If it doesn't, she has little use for the information or event. This woman is easy to recognize. She uses "I," and "me" a lot. She also likes to be the center of attention.

If your strength is small, don't carry heavy burdens. If your words are worthless, don't give advice.
- Chinese Proverb

A self-aware woman, on the other hand, has a much broader view of life and her role in it. She understands her strengths and weaknesses and how they interact with the capabilities and limita-tions of others. She has experienced success and failure and has made some judgments about how to be effective. She is keenly interested in the point of view of others because she enjoys learning. She also knows her hot buttons.

A self-absorbed woman is often a pain in the neck; a woman who is self-aware is easier to be around. A self-centered woman will take great umbrage at being called selfish. A self-assured woman will consider the source.

The word judgmental is used in the same way. The truth is that you and I make judgments every day. We choose coffee over motor oil to drink with our morning toast and put motor oil instead of coffee into our vehicles. We dress one way to go to work and another way to play outside. We choose foods on some basis such as agreeable taste or specific health benefits. We choose to mostly obey the speed limit unless we are late for a meeting. We accept or decline social invitations based on a variety of factors that shape our judgment.

Usually when someone calls another person judgmental, one of three things is at play:

1) She doesn't understand the basis of the judgment that has been made,

2) She disagrees with the judgment, or

3) She objects to the manner in which the judgment is shared.

In each case, the accuser is telling more about herself than about the person she has labeled "judgmental." A wise woman knows this. She does not shy away from making keen judgments based on a consideration of facts and circumstances and matching these with her personal values and preferences.

Then there's the B-word. Twenty years ago, hearing the word "bitch" hurled at a woman was quite shocking. The insult was generally intended to mean that a woman was vile, mean-spirited, overly aggressive, and usually a man-hater. Today, the term has lost its sting.

In fact, embracing BITCH as an acronym, one can find reason to appreciate the epithet. Instead of vile and mean-spirited, think of a BITCH as someone who **B**rings **I**nformation **T**o **C**hange **H**earts. When you think about it, that's often what is going on.

Consider the interactions between moms and teenagers. On any given morning during the school year, moms are waking kids up or listening to alarm clocks go off, perhaps much earlier than during the summer months. Kids naturally object. If you can help your child understand that you are teaching a life skill that will provide a sense of power and pride in later years, you can help change their hearts about this mean demand you make today.

Similarly, when you set boundaries around homework, TV watching, computer use and the like, you help them learn self-discipline and respect for boundaries. This is vital to happiness as an adult. You must maintain the boundaries long enough for them to quit testing and recognize that your expectations are firm and consistent. In addition to helping them form self-standards, this helps them trust you. The next time someone tries to slow you down by calling you a bitch, smile to yourself and thank them for recognizing your true intention.

So those are a few of life's uncomfortable realities. As you know there are scores more. Remember Marcus Aurelius' words: "The first rule is to keep an untroubled spirit. The second is to look things in the face and know them for what they are."

I'll add a few more words. Pay attention to your instincts. Trust your gut. I know that sounds hackneyed and trite because it is said so often. But it is a skill you must practice deliberately. Make it part of developing substance, keeping in mind that you can only live life going forward and you can only understand it looking back.

Timing Is Everything

Should you look for a new job, go back to school, break up with a long-term partner, get your teeth straightened, replace the carpeting, buy a new car, or ask for a raise? Often times, we consider something a risk when what we are really trying to do is decide whether now is the right time to take the leap or let go.

As I mentioned in an earlier chapter, I thought my mother's decision to go back to school was a terrible one at the time she decided to do it. Turns out it was precisely the right time to get

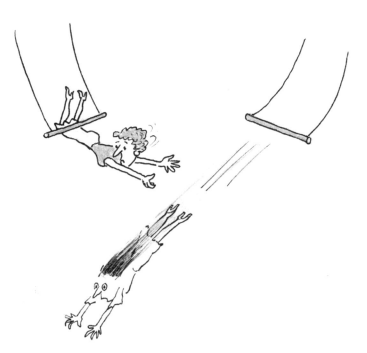

her degree and certification in order to land a job she thoroughly enjoyed.

This question of when to act can be one of the biggest barriers we face. Making a decision to do something is one thing; actually taking steps to do it is something entirely different. You may worry about what others think, whether things will work out the way you hope, whether you have enough money, enough energy to finish what you started, or enough courage to change course if things go awry.

For years, Stephanie wanted to start an independent practice as a coach. She had long and deep experience as a corporate human resources executive and was tired of the daily regimen of waking up early, making the trek to the office, mediating petty spats between people who are old enough to know better, and filing administrative paperwork. She longed to make a bigger difference in people's lives. She longed for the freedom to work on her schedule not her employer's.

She also enjoyed the paycheck she got every two weeks and worried a great deal about how she was going to support herself as an independent. Stephanie spent years building credentials through training her company provided along with external certification programs and continuing education courses. She joked about all the initials she could put behind her name and how if she studied a few years longer she could probably have the entire alphabet represented.

Underneath this near obsession with credentialing, Stephanie was terrified to pull the trigger. It just didn't seem like the right time. The economy was shaky, the kids weren't finished with school, and her employer was still contributing to her 401k account. With one more certification she could offer a service unique to the market. Days turned into weeks turned into months and after nearly ten years of wondering if now was the right time, Stephanie finally decided to take make her move.

Waiting too long can be costly. It makes me sad to hear about women who are getting divorced after thirty years of unhappy marriage saying they wish they had done it twenty years earlier. It makes me mad to hear them blame all their unhappiness on the ex-spouse. Not because I know or care about who they left, but because they are refusing to acknowledge their role in creating so many years of discontent. Women of beauty and substance know that life is full of risk. When they choose to avoid it or protect themselves from it, they own the choice. Same when they decide to go after something they want with no guarantee they will succeed.

The best way to know the time is right to act is to approach a big decision through a series of smaller related decisions. Stephanie could have done coaching work in the evening or on weekends to see if it was indeed something she wanted to do full time. She could have investigated the possibility of working part-time at her company. She could have worked as a temp for an established coaching firm. Each small decision would have provided information to guide her big decision to strike out on her own. This information may have assured and encouraged her; it may have caused her to reconsider her goal.

While waiting too long can be risky, acting too swiftly can be, too. I chuckle to think of my impetuous friend Allie who bounces from one job to another and has had three or four different fiancés over the course of the past eight years. Ironically, she has never married because the time was never right. In truth, she doesn't know what she wants and can't seem to sit still long enough to figure it out. Lately, she is beginning to regret her bohemian ways. She feels like it's time to grow up and get serious about her life. There's that time thing again.

Time passes, things change, and windows of opportunity open and close all around you. Learning to embrace the risk of life, see it for what it is, and choose actions that move you closer to the happiness you seek represents a wonderful journey of discovery. Don't be surprised when, in the midst of it all, you find yourself having a blast. Risk? What's that?

CHAPTER SEVEN

OVERCOMING DISAPPOINTMENT

"Cut him loose!" How often we hear women say this to each other! Whether the situation is a failed relationship, a team member who isn't fulfilling his responsibilities, or a friend who continues to harangue you about something that is old news, the impulse to cut someone off can be semi-automatic. It feels natural. And it may indeed be the right response. But doing so impetuously often brings unintended consequences.

It may affect others who are close to you. It may destroy future opportunities. It may make you look foolish, uninformed, immature, or worse.

The first three words in M. Scott Peck's timeless classic *The Road Less Traveled* are "Life is difficult."

These are words that need to be repeated today. Not once in a while, but often enough so that we understand the truth they hold. Snow is cold. Water is wet. Life is difficult.

What they mean is that we should expect challenge. We should expect struggle. We should expect disappointment. Not all the time or in all things, but certainly sometimes and maybe at the worst times.

It is a royal pain when our clothes get wet in the rain, but we don't expect anything different. We learn to deal with it. We carry umbrellas or wear raincoats to minimize our discomfort and limit damage to clothing. The same is true about life.

We learn to manage unfortunate realities.

Over the past couple of generations, we have turned away from this pragmatism. With decent jobs, good pay, and a burgeoning market of amazing material bounty, we began to expect that life should be easy. Certainly easier than any previous generation knew.

Talented designers in every industry captured the wizardry of technology and made it our servant. We touched a button or a magic screen and goodness sprang forth! Communication, transportation, entertainment, even household maintenance became swift and easy. Such happiness! Such ease!

And now we see the catch. Life really is difficult. The sunny days of better economic times have given way to unanticipated storms. We get angry when things go wrong, when friends lose jobs, and unemployment settles too close to home or stays too long with a loved one. We are offended when someone says something rude. We feel frustrated to a ridiculous degree by little things: a broken fingernail, a sweater caught on something out of place, spilled coffee on skirts or laptops. Such is life. It happens, whether we are in the mood for it or not.

Mostly, we're not. Disappointment is everywhere. And sometimes, I think women are especially attuned to it. Heaven knows we have our reasons.

Face creams that don't erase wrinkles. Surly check-out clerks. Gym memberships that don't make us divas. Spoiled produce. Stale bread. Lousy gas mileage. Depressing weather. Friends and family—family!—who don't get it.

> *If we will be quiet and ready enough, we shall find compensation in every disappointment.*
> - Henry David Thoreau

Clothes that shrink. Computers that crash. Promises that are broken. Years that fly by with no regard for the dreams we once had. Disappointment is an everyday fact of life. Learning to overcome it is a life skill worth honing.

I remember sitting on the back porch of a dear friend's house many years ago. I was pondering divorce and she was a single mom with two sons. She told me two things. "If you can find a way to say married, stay married. It's easier than being a single parent." I couldn't find a way to stay married.

The second thing she told me was, "If you can get used to the idea that everyone in your life—everyone in your life—will disappoint you at some time, you'll be able to handle just about anything."

We had a lengthy conversation about this. I didn't understand what she meant. I could not imagine how certain people in my life could ever disappoint me. It hurt just thinking they might. What I came to understand then, and have experienced many times since, is that people don't deliberately set out to disappoint you. But because they are human and they do what they do, at some point what they do will disappoint you in some way.

Teenage kids leave wads of used chewing gum on the edge of the counter top with the trashcan centimeters away. Friends go on and on about their current dramas, never asking how you are. Bosses accept truly outstanding work you produced on your own time without so much as an acknowledgment, never mind a thank you.

And then take credit for it!

As I was writing this book, I watched the Green Bay Packers lose to the New York Giants in a divisional playoff game. I have been a Packers fan since I was a kid, when guys like Jerry Kraemer, Boyd Dollar, Carroll Dale, Bart Star, Donny Anderson, Paul Hornung, Ray Nitschke, Elijah Pitts and Bobby Jeter were my heroes.

The team went through a terrible trough for years. After beating all odds in 2010 to win on the road throughout the playoffs, make it to the Super Bowl, and then win it, the expectations on the team the following year were sky high. And for the most part, the team responded, winning fifteen games and losing only one all season.

But the team's performance in the playoff game was pathetic. Dropped passes, turnovers, even favorable calls by the referees could not secure a win for the home team. I speak for Packer Nation when I say the disappointment was bitter. Bitter!

The Stories You Tell Yourself

There was a very funny story going around the Internet a couple of years ago. It involved a woman meeting her husband for dinner. She was ten minutes late after spending the afternoon with girlfriends. He greeted her with coolness. She wondered if he was irritated because she was late? It was only ten minutes.

After some stilted conversation, they ordered. When the food came, her husband ate without his usual gusto and seemed preoccupied as she tried to engage him in conversation. Was he sick? Had he lost interest in her? In the car on the way home, she tried again to engage him in conversation. He was quiet. When she told him she loved him, he didn't respond.

By the time the woman went to bed she was in tears. She was certain her husband no longer loved her. She was also certain, as she thought about his behavior in recent weeks, that he was having an affair. She wondered how she would live on her own after he ran off with his girlfriend. What would she tell the kids? Her life as she had known it in 20-plus years of marriage was over.

As her husband came to bed some time later, he was still preoccupied. His boat wouldn't start and he couldn't figure out why.

Every man with whom I share this story laughs out loud. They say their wives or girlfriends are exactly like this. Every woman I share this story with shakes her head in woeful recognition. She has been there, done that. Why?

Why, indeed.

Lacking information, most people create stories to explain what is currently going on from their limited perspective. Uncertainty and even the tiniest bit of insecurity makes these stories personal and often wildly overblown.

The story I told myself about the Packers loss was admittedly overblown.

"This is epic! It should not have happened! This team is bigger than their mistakes! They are steeped in character! They should have pulled together, focused their efforts, and done what they know how to do. (And what they are paid handsomely to do, I might add.) The coaches made foolish calls. Onside kicks? Are you kidding me? Receivers dropped as many passes as they caught. What is wrong with them? The Green Bay Packers lost their first playoff game of 2012, at home!"

I was stunned, angry, frustrated, and keenly disappointed. The stories I told myself made me deeply unhappy! And I had exactly zero control over any aspect of the game or its outcome.

On a much more everyday level, regular people disappoint us, too. Simply by being themselves, people are bound to rub you the wrong way sometimes. Simply by being yourself, you are bound to rub other people the wrong way sometimes. We are all different in our preferences, practices, habits, assumptions and abilities.

Generally speaking, we choose friends who are like us and gravitate toward those who share our perspectives. When they disappoint us, we feel confused and unhappy. Somehow they fall short of our expectations.

Such is life. We suffer disappointment. Our heroes turn out to be only human after all. Our ability to influence an outcome is sometimes equal to zero. The stories we tell ourselves help us deal with disappointment or paralyze us in the face of it.

Marilou and Bridget shared office space for nearly a decade. During this time, they shared many life experiences as well. Their kids went to the same school, they served on the same boards; they socialized together with their husbands. Several years before their lease was due to expire, they began talking informally about the future. In each of those informal conversations, Bridget indicated that she loved their office space and wanted to stay.

However, two months before the lease expired, Bridget sent Marilou an email message stating that she had found new space and would not renew her portion of their shared lease. In the email, Bridget apologized for delivering the message electronically, admitting that she did not want to deal with "a big blowup."

Marilou was furious. She felt betrayed, stabbed in the back, abandoned. In describing her reaction to the email notification, she said she had never been treated so poorly, especially by someone she considered a friend. She was baffled by Bridget's seemingly abrupt about-face, but was angrier still about how Bridget delivered her decision. *An email message? Are you kidding?*

Marilou's reaction was just what Bridget feared. Loud. Angry. Emotional. Judgmental. A big blowup with little room for reasoned dialog.

Marilou felt entirely justified in her hot reaction. A so-called friend of ten years dumps you without enough warning to be able to find different space and make all the necessary professional adjustments including new stationary, phone numbers, and professional membership changes? Did Bridget give one thought to the inconvenience and expense Marilou would have to absorb as a result of her decision?

It is easier to forgive an enemy than to forgive a friend.
- William Blake

Here is where we must stop to consider the stories we tell ourselves.

Marilou's story line went like this. "Bridget has been an office partner for ten years. We have shared personal lives, as well as professional lives, and she promised that she would renew our lease. Bailing out on the lease and telling me via email is an act of brutal betrayal and professional disrespect. I have never been treated so poorly in my whole life!"

We don't know Bridget's story line. For whatever reason, she decided that renewing the lease was not something she wanted to do. She had not made a promise to renew; she merely indicated her desire to do so. Her decision may have had something to do with her relationship with Marilou over the past ten years or it may have had nothing to do with Marilou.

The story Marilou tells herself about the situation guarantees that she will be angry. It prevents her from having a meaningful conversation with Bridget and justifies Bridget's concern about encountering "a big blowup."

Overcoming disappointment is a difficult, often painful, experience. Done well, it sets you apart as a woman of substance, someone who can absorb the barbs of life while maintaining equilibrium and continuing to move forward.

All this takes time! I don't want to suggest for one moment that a woman of beauty and substance bounces back from keen disappointment with a snap of her fingers to the foxy, confident babe that exists in her mind.

Though it may be a silly example, my struggle to overcome disappointment with the Packers loss left me feeling ungrounded. I didn't want to work, I didn't want to talk to anyone, I didn't want to pretend to be okay. I was angry! I know many Packers fans understand these emotions because they have endured them, too.

Yet stepping back a bit, I had to chuckle at myself. I have experienced these feelings since I was a child. After a Packers loss then, I would run down the hallway to my room and slam the door to cry in private. My father, a Chicago Bears fan, would ask my mother, "What's wrong with that kid?" Nothing other than a deep reservoir of passion for my football team!

Football aside, there are aspects of my life with which I am sorely disappointed. But I have also been privileged to live an interesting and instructive life. My work has taken me to many places away from home and introduced me to thousands of unique and intriguing individuals. Memories are too numerous to count.

I suspect your life is the same. Surely, there are parts that make you shake your fist in fury or your head in sadness. Just as surely, there are parts that make you smile all the way to your toes. The stories you choose to tell yourself will either warm and strengthen you or make you bitter and fragile. Women of beauty and substance choose stories that build and reject stories that diminish. It is a choice, though not an easy one.

Beware the Wallow

You know this beast. It wakes up when you begin to feel sorry for yourself. You're sick again. Your team lost. You missed the train to work because one of the kids forgot his homework. Your partner doesn't pay the kind of attention to you he once did. The more irritants you can identify, the more energized the wallow becomes.

Your feet hurt. You're tired all the time. Your favorite restaurant messed up your favorite meal. The waiter was rude. The restaurant was cold. The music was too loud. The beast rises up, stretches, and gets ready for a good run, fueled by your pessimism.

When you launch into your standard litany, the beast takes off, pulling you in its wake. "No one can truly understand my suffering because no one I know has ever been where I've been or endured my pain. Because no one can understand, the suggestions they offer about how to get better don't work. They just don't apply to me. Someday maybe I'll figure out how to be happy again, but I doubt it."

If you have ever had a friend like this, you know how difficult it is to talk with her. Nothing you say or do will convince her that life can be better in the future. Stuck in her wallow, she refuses to see beyond her pain. Self-pity never leads to beauty or substance. It is a waste of time and energy.

The wallow is a terrible trap! It turns a routine pity party into a gigantic blues bash. But this party has no guests. It's just you on a runaway rant. The wallow is a very, very bad habit.

Brenda was newly divorced when she decided to explore online dating. She wrote a charming profile and selected a photo taken some years earlier at a family reunion. She glowed with happiness! She posted her profile and photo to several dating sites and was thrilled as winks and invitations to exchange email and phone calls came flooding in. Brenda was newly energized! Maybe after the past few years of unhappiness, she would find true love again. And this time it would be true love! She had learned from her mistakes.

> *Longed for him.*
> *Got him.*
> *Shit.*
>
> - Margaret Atwood

After speaking with a variety of men, Brenda agreed to meet a select few for lunch, drinks and in one case, a walk after work. Finding an interested and sympathetic ear among some of these men, she began to tell stories of her unhappy marriage and divorce. Most of the men, also divorced, could relate. Brenda sounded just like their ex-wives! She wallowed in the misery of injustices done, sad misunderstandings that might have been corrected if only her husband knew how to listen, and a vow never to be taken advantage of again.

Guess how many second dates Brenda had. And guess how she responded. Yes, she wallowed some more.

A wallow is a perpetual complaint and pity party that gets stuck on unhappy and sucks the energy out of anyone it encounters. A wallow destroys a woman's sense of self as it slouches toward the future carrying a heavy sack of sadness. It is like quicksand because the more you feel like you want to escape but talk about why you're there, the deeper you sink. The only way out is to stop talking and start thinking about what you want to do next.

We all have dark days. When you have several in a row, you may begin to wonder what is wrong with you. Maybe it is something you are doing or maybe it is just a string of unfortunate luck. If you can analyze the situation objectively, you might come to a conclusion that restores your spirit and allows you to emerge from the funk.

That's a six-foot "if." Normally, when you are in a funk and start thinking about what's wrong, your thoughts serve to prolong the funk. You may hear yourself talking about all the things that are not working, forgetting that there are some things that are.

Keeping a gratitude journal is a good way to counteract the wallow. Stopping yourself mid-whine is another. Telling yourself "stop it" when you find yourself focusing on negativity is still another. I have a dear friend who says out loud, "Satan get away from me!" when she feels herself wanting to complain. Her husband chuckles when he hears her walking down the hall berating Satan. He admires her strength.

Defeating the wallow takes discipline. It means you have to forgo the urge to tell others about how difficult your life is and instead turn your thoughts and words toward more positive and productive ends. This can be very difficult to do when you just wish someone would carry your load for a little while. Make up your mind to be stronger than sadness.

Be strict with yourself when it comes to complaining. Force yourself to change the mental channel. Yes, it will feel artificial. Jenny told me one day that although she loves me as a friend, I am one of her biggest pains in the you-know-what because I won't get off this happiness thing. I annoy her every time she complains about her husband or job and I change the subject.

She wants to smack me, strangle me, or just tell me to go away. It's painful for her to give up her misery; I can see that. But the only way she will begin to build some trust in herself and a future that is even slightly better than the wallow fest she lives is to start small.

That's true for the rest of us as well.

As the year 2012 was winding down, I found myself in a delightful conversation with a woman at New York's LaGuardia airport, where our flight had been delayed by several hours due to weather. As the woman approached the vacant seat next to mine, she seemed to hesitate. I looked up from the book I was reading, smiled and moved my briefcase to provide more room. A stout woman, she was dressed completely in black; her hair was pulled back and tucked under a knitted black hat. She parked her luggage, stood looking around the area for a few minutes, then asked if I would watch her things while she went for a cup of tea. I told her I would be happy to do so.

When she came back, she settled into the seat and asked if I was going to Milwaukee for a visit or returning home. Thus began a fascinating conversation. I learned that she had been born in Milwaukee, but had lived in Brooklyn nearly 40 years. She was an orthodox Jew, had eight children and was expecting her 30th grandchild. She arranged flowers for weddings and attended every one to congratulate the bride and groom and visit a short while with the families. She loved her neighborhood because it was full of children and constantly buzzing with activity.

She was on her way to Milwaukee to visit her father, who was in a nursing home. He is 86 years old and frail. Her sister lives in Brown Deer. She doesn't think she could live "west" anymore—it is too quiet.

The woman graduated one year ahead of me in high school, adopted orthodox beliefs in her early 20s, and has been married to her first husband for 36 years. She doesn't know what has gone wrong with young people today.

At this point in her soliloquy, I began to wonder if engaging her in conversation had been a mistake. I wondered if I would have any chance to get back to my reading. Mostly, I wondered if I was going to have to endure a tirade on religion.

I needn't have worried. She told me that she wanted her email address to be tickleyourownarmpit, but it is too long. When I gave her a puzzled look, she said the trouble with young people today—especially young women—is that they go looking for someone who can make them happy. "Marriage isn't about finding someone to make you happy," she said, "it is about finding someone you can trust."

"Love isn't about getting all sparkly, although that is nice, especially at the start. It is about putting up with irritations, having the courage to stand up for yourself in an argument, and being willing to hug someone you'd just as soon spit at."

I chuckled in agreement.

She continued. "Telling someone goodbye 'because I don't love you anymore' is foolish. Girls need to understand that they're gonna get mad at their husbands. They'll remember old boyfriends. They'll wonder if their real prince is still somewhere out there waiting. But none of this is worth dwelling on because someone at home needs your understanding, special recipe or a hug."

"And believe me, that cute guy over there is going to turn into a big lout like every other man. It's just what happens to them."

At this, I laughed out loud.

"You doubt me?" she asked.

I still chuckle at the unlikely conversation. Here was a woman as different from me as could be in appearance, upbringing, demeanor, background, education, and life experience, and we wholeheartedly agree that you have to learn to find ways to make yourself happy. No one—not husband, best friend, or dear family member—is in charge of this important aspect of life. Your happiness is up to you. Wallowing is a self-imposed and self-destructive sentence.

So whether it is a fine cup of tea, favorite TV program, beautiful sunset, the song of a bird in the yard, or a good laugh with a crazy friend, find ways to give yourself a boost without making someone else responsible. Tickle your own armpit.

Forgiveness is a Power Play

One of the most challenging aspects of overcoming disappointment is making a decision to forgive the one who disappointed you. Whether that person purposely hurt you or, as is often the

case, made a mistake that offended you, you always have the choice to forgive.

Health and happiness experts agree that in order to let go of the past and heal from its wounds, you must forgive. "Forgive and forget."

Yet many women struggle with this advice. My friend, Lois, says she can forgive, but she will not forget. She does not want to keep making the same mistakes. Fair enough. How about "forgive and release." Forgive both the person who hurt you and yourself for being involved in the first place. Then release both of you from the energy of bad feelings. Take the lesson; leave the hurt behind.

> *The weak can never forgive. Forgiveness is the attribute of the strong.*
> - Mahatma Gandhi

Some women believe, mistakenly, that if they do not let the offender know how terribly hurt they are by the offender's words or actions, transgressors will walk all over them. Expressing loud indignation is a sure way, they believe, to let the culprit know such behavior will not be tolerated and that an apology is expected.

Whether or not this approach produces an apology, it is not likely to change the offender's behavior in any significant way. Instead, a loud objection reinforces the stereotype of women who are oversensitive and prone to drama.

For those less inclined to take a loud and public stand, an alternative strategy is to tell everyone but the transgressor that you will not stand for such behavior. This strategy reinforces the stereotype of women who are timid and whiney. Neither offers forgiveness.

Marlene is a smart, successful, professional woman in her mid-forties. She enjoys membership in an exclusive group of equally successful women who range in age from late-30s to mid-60s and live in a major metropolitan area. They are power players in their industries and their community. They are proud of themselves and each other. They refer to one another as friends.

One day, the group met for lunch to celebrate a promotion won by one of their members. Marlene was out of town and therefore unaware that her friends had met. In fact she did not hear about it until some months later. When she did, she called a friend to ask about the lunch. "Oh, it was wonderful! Maribeth was thrilled with her promotion and so happy to meet us all at her favorite restaurant for lunch."

"Why wasn't I invited?" Marlene asked.

"What do you mean? I thought you were out of town."

"I was. But nobody told me about the lunch. Nobody asked me if I could come. I didn't even know about Maribeth's promotion until I read it online. What's going on?"

An awkward silence hung between them for several seconds, which was long enough for Marlene to decide she had been betrayed and abandoned by her friends. She mentally searched her behavior trying to figure out what she had done to offend the group. Finding nothing, she decided that her friends were disloyal, egotistical, and superficial and that friendship held no meaning for them. Marlene separated from the group.

Years later, Marlene still talks about the incident. She carries the hurt and confusion as a reminder that people are not always what they seem and that few are to be trusted.

Marlene has the first part of that right. People are not always what they seem. In fact, unless you take time to truly know people, they are rarely what they seem. We define people by our perceptions, assumptions, and experiences, then either celebrate them when they accidentally match our views or get hurt by them when they behave differently. Isn't it ironic how we can hurt ourselves without really trying?

The second part, that few people are to be trusted, is a choice. I have found in many years of working with people, that those who choose to distrust others are generally operating from a lack of self-trust or self-confidence.

Women of beauty and substance do not invest inordinate amounts of time worrying about whom to trust. They accept people for who they are, form relationships with those who have common interests, and assume full responsibility for their own lives. When hurt, they know that forgiveness is a power play. This is because they recognize that in forgiving someone who has disappointed them, they gain freedom to continue on life's path unencumbered by the pain of a broken heart.

I know this sounds simple and logical. I also know from experience it is excruciatingly difficult and sometimes outrageously emotional.

Being dumped by a lover or fired from a job are two of the quintessential disappointments a woman can face. After investing precious time and tons of energy and devotion dreaming of a 'happily ever after' with another wonderful human, her world shatters to pieces when the lover says goodbye.

"Hell hath no fury like a woman scorned," derived from William Congreve's writing, in *The Mourning Bride*, 1697, captures the nature of a woman's reaction to dismissal.

So does my friend Amy's anguished question: "How are you supposed to forgive someone who promises you the world, then abruptly skedaddles?"

Losing a job unexpectedly can also call forth mind wracking and ultimately futile questions. What did I do? What didn't I do?

Who threw me under the bus? What lies have been told? Why me?

The time and energy spent trying on your own to figure out what happened is pure waste. If you can have a conversation with someone in position to answer your questions, do so. However, be prepared to hear superficial answers, dodges, or excuses. This is an extremely uncomfortable conversation that can get people in legal trouble. At the end of it all, what will you have gained?

Go back and read this chapter again. People will disappoint you. It is a fact of life. The stories you tell yourself about the disappointment will help you get better or make you sick. Wallowing in your hurt and anger will surely destroy many days and may lead you to unhealthy coping behaviors. Learning to forgive frees you to move forward to embrace with optimism whatever comes next.

Forgiveness is a power play that has nothing to do with the offender. It has everything to do with you making a choice to carry on with your life. Grieving a loss takes time. Be patient with yourself. But make up your mind to forgive those who hurt you. They have moved on. You should, too.

Acknowledge and Move On

I was sitting on the living room floor with my two daughters, a big bowl of popcorn in front of us. We had just settled in for an evening of sharing the day's experiences, something we all loved to do. My day at work had been unusually challenging. I was at wit's end about a particular employee who had been problematic for years. He could not seem to do what he said, despite a knack for the business and all the support he could need. He did not return phone calls. He was late to meetings. He consistently missed deadlines. But he earnestly promised to be better. Always he promised to be better.

After nearly a half hour of ranting about this individual, my youngest daughter, who was ten years old at the time, turned to me, munched on a few kernels of popcorn and said, "Mom. Acknowledge and move on."

I was astonished at her words and laughed heartily in appreciation. How did she come up with that? She must have heard it on TV! Even so, her perfect application of advice to the conversation was impressive.

I've never forgotten it. And I don't think there are four more powerful words of advice when you are struggling to overcome disappointment. *Acknowledge and move on.*

Simple words, big act. Before you can acknowledge something, you must see it. This involves looking life directly in the face and recognizing what you see. This can take extraordinary strength! Sometimes you don't want to be an adult. Sometimes you want to wallow, make people pay for what they did to you, or refuse to see what is in front of you.

Women who refuse to see children abusing drugs, engaging in early sexual activity, or participating in violence do not change the behavior. They do limit their effectiveness as parents. And sometimes they lose their children.

Katherine, a well-known and well-regarded executive, confessed to friends over lunch one day that her grade-school son was showing up at school drunk. The principal had called the day before to tell her. She was shocked, angry, scared and at a complete loss about what to do. She was afraid to tell her husband. What kind of mother would he think she is? And besides that, if she talked about it, it would become too real. Maybe if she kept the news to herself, she could pretend this was a little prank or a normal exploration of boundaries.

But she knew better. She said she noticed some months ago that he started taking an extra bottle of orange juice on the bus.

Never in her wildest dreams had she considered something like this. Not her son! Truthfully, she said she began to notice little changes in his behavior; nothing big and nothing out of the ordinary for boys approaching puberty. She tried to ignore it and quiet the bad feelings in her stomach by leaving earlier for work. She was confident at work. She had control over many things and a reputation of which she was justifiably proud.

When you forgive,
you in no way
change the past —
but you sure do
change the future.
- Bernard Meltzer

Fortunately, this story has a happy ending. Katherine did talk with her husband and together they approached the boy. Over the course of several months' work with a therapist, they learned a lot about each other, their needs and how they could support one another going forward. They emerged stronger. Not without fear, struggle and a great many tears, which often come with acknowledgment of reality. This pain is what holds many back from seeing what's really there.

You may be one of those unfortunate souls who has learned to forgive everyone but yourself. In a recent conversation about this, a woman asked with tears in her eyes how she can possibly forgive all the mistakes she has made in her life. She can forgive others and let go of any hurt she suffered at their hands. But she knows too much about her dark past to truly forgive herself.

This is a sad truth for many people. No matter how kind they are now, how religious, how much penance they have done, or how patient, generous or helpful they are to others, they just can't shake their own judgment.

The science test you flunked in middle school that was the final straw in breaking your chance to enter med school? Let it go. That fight you had with your brother-in-law, now deceased, that wracks you with guilt every time you think about it? Let it go. That job you quit that you now realize you should have kept? Let it go.

It's all history. None of it can be changed. It is part of you and, properly understood, serves as testimony to your strength and determination. Why do you allow certain chapters of your life to darken today and the rest of your days? It doesn't make any sense. There is nothing in self-loathing to build upon. It's all negative and destructive. Your guilt, suffering and stubborn refusal to forgive yourself have no impact whatsoever on any past events. The only person who is hurting from any of them is you. Don't do that.

Acknowledge your past and the pain you feel. Then move on. Your health, happiness and well-being are determined in part by the boundaries you place on your willingness to see truth. If you are unwilling or unable to see the unvarnished reality of life, you will limit your ability to deal with it. Part of this unvarnished reality is that you are a mortal human being who makes mistakes, even when you most ardently wish not to.

As mentioned at the beginning of this book, substance is born of painful experience. Working through life's challenges creates resilience, perspective and a quiet power. These help you acknowledge and move on. They invite you to abandon the habit of grousing about something. They help you change your story, change your tune, change your behavior and get to a different better place. They help you remember that life is difficult and you have the courage to experience it in all its reality.

Movement is an essential element in overcoming disappointment. Getting stuck is bad for your psyche and your physique. Acknowledge and move on.

CHAPTER 8
LIVING THE DREAM

I f you have been reading this book from the beginning, you may now have a head full of ideas, a heart full of trepidation, and some uncertainty about what to do next. If that's the case, rest assured, it is normal.

If you have a few ideas, a passion to start a new way of thinking and living, and a next step or two outlined, get going! Momentum will build as you put one foot in front of the other on your way to what's next.

In this last chapter together, I want to encourage you to imagine the ideal you being truly happy. You are beautiful and strong in ways you always knew you could be. You can create a plan for your life that allows you the flexibility to learn, grow and change course if that's what you decide to do. You can go anywhere you want and you take your place with grace.

You know exactly what to do to be taken seriously and you have become skillful at letting others be. You embrace risk with anticipation and a positive expectation for success. You know how to deal with the inevitable disappointments that will come your way and you are not troubled by mistakes you and others close to you are sure to make. You are living the dream.

What are the three words that describe this truly happy you? Write them down. These are the words you will practice as a woman of beauty and substance, a woman with a backbone.

You may be thinking, "Oh, no. I'm not going to play that game. I know I can't do all those things and I'm not going to try and fail. I may not be totally happy—who is?—but I'm okay." This may be defeatism. Or it may be wisdom.

I have learned over the past several decades of working with people that the word dream is not universally positive. As my friend and colleague Claire so poignantly said one day, "Dreams can cause broken hearts." And so they can if that's the story you tell yourself.

A small child at a Texas charter school once told me that his mother cried when he told her he had a dream to go to college. He told her he wanted to graduate from college so he could get a good job and build her a new house. He promised her she could paint the rooms any color she wanted and he would build a garage big enough for her car and his truck. He wanted her to be excited and happy; her tears made him sad. "But she's okay now," he concluded.

The boy did not understand that his mother's tears came from a heart full of pride, cautious joy, and a hope that might have caused her heart to burst if she let it fully blossom. He could not know that the dream he described had lain dormant in her own soul for most of her life. Wiping away her tears, she gave him a reassuring hug and encouraged him to keep working on it.

Once upon a time, this chapter would have been easier to write. Just a few short generations ago, The Dream was something most people understood and aspired to.

When I was growing up, it meant having the freedom and opportunity to create a life that led to personal happiness. Yes, this included some measure of personal wealth and in my middle -class upbringing I understood that to mean ownership of a modest home and a steady job that paid enough to support a family and go on vacation once in a while. In our home, it sometimes included having a dog. That was a big deal.

As our society has evolved, the meaning of The Dream has morphed. Maybe metastasized is a better analogy. Innovation and globalization introduced us to new products, services, cultures, ideas, religions, and lifestyles. Money became an essential element in realizing The Dream. Becoming a millionaire in this context was a logical goal.

Today, in the second decade of the 21st century, it seems that becoming a millionaire is an expected aspiration, though the route by which a person might get there ranges from winning the lottery to having your own Reality TV show to winning American Idol or manipulating stock market trades. The emphasis has surely shifted from a willingness to work hard and enjoy modest fruits to becoming famous and having a lot of money.

What's odd is that even though there are more millionaires than ever in the history of the world, the level of personal unhappiness seems to be higher than ever, too. In recent years we have seen a constriction in jobs, money, and opportunity. You hear people talk about getting by or making ends meet. About holding onto a job. About not taking chances until things get better.

Oddly, this reminds me a little bit about how I grew up. My parents were careful with their time and money. Restaurant meals were rare and always appreciated as a special birthday treat. My siblings and I wore hand-me-downs, which of course we all hated, but managed to get over. And every day brought new chances to learn, to imagine, to challenge ourselves in school and sports and with our neighborhood kickball games.

I think it's time to turn away from an artificial, socially and financially driven definition of success back to the real notion of a dream, which is imagining yourself as a happy, successful person, free to develop and use your talents to create a life of personal satisfaction. It takes you home, away from the bright lights and inflated expectations of a culture in trouble, and allows you to reflect, plan, and dream. What is your dream?

Yours, Not Theirs

Maybe you are like Donna. Donna holds her dreams close, afraid to let anyone else see them in case they might make fun of her. She doesn't want to hear someone say, "What makes you think you can do that? Why should you have what you want when so many others never will?"

Like a lot of women today, Donna is confused about what she should want or what is even okay to want in a world that seems jealous of success, no matter how hard a person has worked to achieve it. Donna tells me she has more to offer—more energy, more ideas, more love. But nobody has time to see or hear Donna and she lacks the support to explore her talents. So she molds herself to the current image of success and hopes for the best.

Dreams are precious. And they are heartbreakingly fragile. For this reason, most women hold them close, reluctant to share them with anyone but their closest friend or lover. When they do share, they tend to do so with great hesitation. And most often they share in fragments. If the easiest part of the dream seems okay to the other person, maybe the next part of it is okay to share, too. But the minute they detect any sign of disapproval or rejection, the dream goes back into the lock box and shoved under the bed.

If you are like most of the rest of us, you have a lot of people in your life who think they know better than you do what your dream should be.

Watch Little League baseball, Junior League hockey, or a Club sport of any kind and you'll see parents popping veins in their necks or foreheads screaming about the contest. Their kid was fouled. Their kid made a play nobody saw. Or their kid screwed up in a way that embarrassed and infuriated Mom or Dad. What you're seeing is Mom and Dad's dreams being superimposed on their kids' performance. It's never pretty.

To a lesser extent, extended family members, mentors, even high school guidance counselors can steer you in directions that are not quite right for you. They do it with the best of intentions and a sincere desire to help. But your dream is yours, not theirs.

In eighth grade, I wanted to be a lawyer. I earnestly shared this aspiration with my parents, who dismissed my dream because there was no way to support it financially. I was forced to reconsider. My next dream was to be a journalist. When I went back with a request to study journalism, Mom and Dad agreed that this was probably something I would be good at, but again let me know that there was no money to make it happen. They explained reality to me. I had three brothers, each of whom would be expected to support a family. In order to do this, it was assumed that they would go to college, get a degree and marry the girl of their dreams (their dreams!) who would bless them with progeny to carry on the family name.

All of this was very difficult for me to understand, and I tried for many years to live up to someone else's dream of what my life should be like. Employers appreciated 'talents' I didn't really have. Husbands (yes, plural) saw things in me that burnished their reputations, but didn't do much for me.

It took me a very long time to recognize and then acknowledge that I was listening and responding to the dreams other people had for me. I wanted to prove that their belief in me was right! I was worthy of their admiration! I wanted them to know that I appreciated their attention and their consideration. What I did not understand was that I was putting me on the back burner. I was letting my dream take a back seat to theirs. What a mistake!

But I didn't know how to think about my dream. Truth be told, it was fuzzy for a long time. For a while I wanted to be in a rock band. Why? I loved music and dancing—I used to crank up the volume of the radio in my bedroom and dance for hours! Pragmatically, I figured if I was going to make money doing something I loved, I'd better find a band. Trouble was, I had no singing talent, no opportunity for theater or dance training, and I couldn't imagine telling my parents I wanted to do something so frivolous.

I recently spoke to a woman who put away her dream to be an actress or singer because it wasn't practical. The difference is that she has a spectacular voice and a theater degree. After working two years as a fund developer for a major metropolitan symphony orchestra, she decided to dust off her dream. As fate would have it, she was poking around on the Internet one weekend, checking out local bands, when she ran across an ad for a female vocalist. She admits she went back to the ad four or five times. A wide range of emotions swept through her as she imagined herself answering the ad. She felt excited, nervous, silly, bold, washed up, determined, and rebellious before finally thinking, "Well, why not?"

She met the band members, auditioned, and landed the gig. Her eyes sparkle as she tells the story, shaking her head at the unlikelihood of it all. It has renewed her energy, reordered her calendar for practice and performances, and strangely enough, made her job less stressful. She has a new perspective on life and proof that it is never too late to realize a dream.

> *You are never too old to set another goal or dream a new dream.*
>
> - C. S. Lewis

Your dream is precious. It will wait for you if it has to. How can you bring it back to life if you killed it long ago? How can you begin to understand what it might be if you've never given it serious thought? Give yourself permission to imagine that totally happy you we discussed earlier. Forget about the opinions or judgment of others. What you want to do is different from what anyone else has already done. As you seek to give form to your dream, give careful consideration to these three questions:

What gifts have you been given? From impossibly perfect skin or an athletic physique to a knack for dealing with sick animals or landing helicopters, you have a suite of gifts that is totally unique. Inventory them.

How can you develop these gifts? Forget about what other people think you should do or what the world thinks you should be interested in. Given your talents and aspirations, how do you want to deepen your skill and broaden your experience?

What contribution do you want to make? When all is said and done, what impact would you like your life to have made? What story do you want it to tell?

This last question runs counter to our current culture. Society today would ask you to imagine what riches might be available to you by identifying and developing your unique gifts. Pop culture asks how you might leverage your gifts to acquire more of life's treasures.

But when a dream is yours—not theirs—you get to define the benefits of realizing it. We know from experience with thousands of people that making a contribution or leaving something of value is important.

Here is one of my favorite quotes from Ralph Waldo Emerson, one of my favorite writers, that captures the notion of contribution:

"To laugh often and much;
To win the respect of intelligent people
and the affection of children;
To earn the appreciation of honest critics
and endure the betrayal of false friends;
To appreciate beauty, to find the best in others;
To leave the world a bit better,
whether by a healthy child, a garden patch,
or a redeemed social condition;
To know even one life has breathed easier
because you have lived.
This is to have succeeded."

And from a plaque that hangs in my bathroom:

THAT WOMAN IS A SUCCESS

Who has an appreciation of the world around her
and her unique place in it...
Who has the capacity to give of herself
and to accept graciously the gifts of others...
Who has a commitment to both her work
and the time she sets aside for play...
Who has the enthusiasm to welcome each new day
with warmth and joy and love.

Play To Your Strengths

At the very outset of this book, we considered the notion of envy, namely the envy of other women's physical or intellectual assets. We talked about how wasteful it is to try to be someone you are not. We pick up the conversation again here.

You were born with a constellation of attributes no one else has ever had. No one has your eye color combined with your hip measurements combined with your scientific intellect combined with your ability to make ends meet on virtual economic fumes. No one has ever seen the world the way you see it. No one has ever had quite the dysfunctional family you live in. No one has ever seen the promise of a sunrise the way you have seen it.

No one has felt your fears, dreamed your dreams, sung your happy songs, or cried your tears. You're doing all of it for the very first time. So is your sister. And your friend. Your Mom. Dad. Grandma. Your teacher. Your co-worker. The minister at your church. The mailman. The cashier at the grocery store. The young woman who is earning her way through grad school working with dolphins.

Your dentist. The garbage collector. Your accountant. The kid who takes tickets at your local cinema. The toddler down the street who loves to show you his mittens. The guy in the wheelchair who lost his legs in Afghanistan.

Every person you meet has a different set of strengths and perspective on life. You probably give them all a measure of respect—at least until you know too much about them to be impressed. Family members, especially.

If you were to take a week to observe the most successful of them, you would probably see that they do more of what they are good at and less of what they are not. Unless, that is, they have someone encouraging them to improve their weaknesses. Marcus Buckingham and Donald O. Clifton's book, *Now Discover Your Strengths* lays out a strong case for why bolstering your weakness is never going to be as powerful as playing to your strengths. And yet we are often counseled to shore up areas of weakness if we want to be more successful.

I'm with Marcus and Donald. Find someone to do the things you don't do well. I hire an accounting firm to do my taxes not because my tax situation is terribly complicated but because numbers are my nemesis. I decided that many years ago and I own it. Joni hires a cleaning service because she loves a spotless home but she is an incurable slob. No apologies necessary. Go with your gifts.

Play to your strengths. Develop them purposefully and leverage them to build your dream. Don't worry about looking left or right to see if other people are doing what you're doing. Your dreams are not their dreams and the way they do life, while it may be interesting, is a distraction when you are on a mission to live your dream.

You Don't Need Permission

Speaking of not looking left or right and not worrying about what other people are doing—or what opinions they might have about what you are doing—there is an important truth to be understood as you strive to live your dream. You do not need anyone else's permission. Truly, you don't!

Some women, believing it is still a man's world or feeling annoyed or intimidated by outspoken women, hesitate to share their view of the world, hold back on contributing their strengths, and pooh-pooh the value of their experience. They wait for permission to share what they know. They wait for permission to speak. Sometimes they wait for permission to live the way they want to live.

You may have been taught from the time you were a little girl that this deference was polite. It was the right thing to do if you wanted to be liked, accepted and maybe eventually admired.

With respect and appreciation for this training—I understand where it came from and why and the benefits it conferred on a civil society—I hereby challenge it.

You don't need permission to live your life. In fact, waiting for permission diminishes the value of what you know through experience. Waiting for permission gives someone who doesn't know what you know the power to accept your contribution or set it aside because it is unfamiliar and perhaps uncomfortable.

> *Write yourself a permission slip to be surprised by someone's potential. Who knows? One day that person could be you.*
> *- Sherri Shepherd*

Let's think about this. Somewhere along the way, you may have decided that what certain people know and have experienced is more impressive or important than what you have learned or experienced. I suppose in certain contexts this may be the case. Would it not also be true, however, that in certain contexts your knowledge and experience would be superior to theirs? Perhaps you have never considered this.

If, in addition, these certain people have also convinced others of their superior viewpoint, they may have become powerful to some degree. No one can have power unless others grant it. How many of these people asked for permission? Likely, none!

As you think about living your dream, you would be wise to reflect on your need to have permission from people you care about in order to move ahead. Surely you want support, but support is very different from permission. Even if those closest to you cannot or choose not to support you in pursuing your dream, you can continue on anyway. You don't need their permission. A lack of support from people you care about is not necessarily a personal attack on what you want to do. They may be preoccupied with other issues or unaccustomed to supporting anything that does not serve their immediate interests. Okay. Accepting reality for what it is, you acknowledge and move on to find others who will support you. They are out there!

Be clear about the kinds of support you want and need. Do you want introductions to people in position to help you directly? Do you want someone who will listen as you describe your dream and ask questions to help clarify it? Do you want someone to help uncover your blind spots? Do you want someone to offer you psychological high fives as encouragement to forge ahead? All of this assistance is available.

The Power of Laughter

One of the most powerful exercises in my workshops is plotting a journey line and sharing life stories—the high points, low points and lessons learned along the way.

It is typical for people to hesitate as they consider what to share. Am I bragging if I share too many high points? Am I willing to risk vulnerability in sharing real low points? How honest are others going to be?

As we look back on life so far and remember stories we have made with family, friends, clients, and strangers, we see the remarkable power of laughter to heal and re-energize. Often, this laughter comes after sharing something uncomfortable or even painful.

As a freshman in high school, I got busted in a library conversation with a friend referring to an algebra teacher as "Square Root DeGroot." Who popped up over the library carrel to catch me in the act? Mr. DeGroot himself! I happened to be in his class at the time. Not only was I mortified; I was scared that his irritation would find its way into my grade. Moments after the incident happened, my friend and I were gasping for air in the midst of our laughter.

If you have ever spent time around little girls (or women drinking wine), you know the hilarity and fun of a case of the giggles. It is one of my favorite experiences with my granddaughters. Something tickles someone's funny bone and a giggle bubbles up. The sound of the giggle tickles someone else's funny bone and she joins in. The sight and sound of several people laughing causes others to start to giggle. Soon we are all laughing, though we're not sure why! By the time we have laughed ourselves out, we feel deliciously tired and so happy about being together. We have shared magic.

To experience a truly refreshing laugh, you have to let yourself go. You have to forget about who might be watching, what your face might look like and whether or not you might let out a snort. (Kel, that little snort is one of your most endearing qualities!) Laughter makes you forget for the moment any disagreements, insults, or resentments. Laughter clears the air and lightens the soul. But you have to give in to it in order to experience its power.

My friend and colleague, Donna "Kinza" Christenson, teaches laughter workshops. She has done extensive research on the power of laughter and shares it unselfishly with whoever wants to learn and let go. She tells stories of how reticence turns to enjoyment when people experience the sheer goodness of a genuine belly laugh, sometimes for the first time in a very long time.

Finding the humor in everyday life takes some practice. Appreciating the variety of interesting hairdos people sport is always good for a silent chuckle. No real hair could be that color or hold that shape! Watching angry people gesture or happy people sing in their cars; noticing how the wind causes people to grab at hats and clothes and newspapers; seeing toddlers running helter skelter and laughing along the way... life is filled to the brim with reasons to laugh.

Catching yourself doing silly things is also a good way to lighten up. Rather than turning on the hallway light in the pre-dawn darkness, I bump my heel against the stair to make sure it is there before stepping down. Why? I don't know; I just do it.

Why do you leave three drops of milk in the carton and return it to the fridge? Why does everyone say, "Oh, no, you eat the last cookie," instead of accepting it with a smile? Why, when you are cleaning, do you pick up a piece of fuzz to see what it is, then drop it on the floor and suck it up with the vacuum cleaner?

Why do you say, "What?" when you heard what the other person said? Why does your teenager test your patience in ways the neighbor's teenager doesn't? Why does the dog wrap itself around the tree and bark to be released only when it is raining or snowing? Why, when the car needs gas, do you wait until the next day to see if gas prices will be lower only to inevitably find that they went up overnight?

Change your opinions, keep to your principles; change your leaves, keep intact your roots.
- Victor Hugo

When you decide to work on your dream, you may feel anxious; surely you will feel some level of uncertainty, perhaps even doubt. This is normal and good. There is energy in anxiety! Learn to capture it and use it to propel yourself forward. Laughter is a wonderful way to release this energy, clear your mind and heart, and provide important rest. Find reasons each day to laugh a little.

Remember my story about speaking before a large audience of educated, successful women? The one where I completely lost my train of thought? What a grand laugh we had! And how grateful I am that I was not 20- or 30-something years old. I remember taking myself much more seriously back then, trying in earnest to live up to the expectations I thought others had of me. That's a wicked trap that is easy to fall into and tough to get out of. The good news: if you live long enough, make enough mistakes, and laugh hard enough, you can spring the trap.

Patience, Persistence, and Practice

Perhaps it is fitting to follow a quick discussion of laughter with a prescription for learning to become a woman of beauty and substance on your terms and in your time. Your ultimate goal is to generate goodness and a genuinely happy life for yourself and those you care about.

This journey is not easy. Pledging to acknowledge reality and work through disappointment without making others pay for the pain they have caused you is akin to sainthood in some people's books. It's hard to argue the point sometimes.

Cutting people slack when your expectations exceed their current capability can seem like mission impossible or worse, a dereliction of duty. Understanding the audience you're playing to is imperative.

The point of this book and the *Backbone Guide* series generally is to remind you of the three elements of Backbone: Competence, Confidence, and Risk-Taking; that building competence takes time; that confidence is sometimes a lagging indicator of competence so persistence of effort is key; and that action is where it all finds meaning.

Patience is possible when you know your desired outcome and believe you have the capability to get there. Not necessarily by next Tuesday at noon, but someday.

Persistence is the dogged effort to put one foot in front of the other despite snow storms, typhoons, broken promises, betrayed friendships, wardrobe malfunctions and myriad and sundry other setbacks. Sometimes it's wise to disengage brain and work the plan. Too much ruminating can lead to all sorts of creative excuses for why it is time to stop pursuing a dream.

Risk-taking is all about action. **Practice.** Risks don't have to be big hairy audacious life or death propositions. They can involve speaking the truth to a loved one in a quiet moment over coffee. They can mean sharing research that suggests a different conclusion than the team has previously reached. And a million other examples of breaking the frame of assumption.

Taking a risk can be as simple and profound as listening to your own heart and taking action based on what you most want to do. It's the action taking that matters. Practicing the things your ideal self would do in any situation. Recording what you want to achieve, the things you try, and the reactions that occur.

If there is one aspect of Backbone that truly changes lives, it is the action of risk taking. We can become very accomplished at understanding the things we need to get better at (competence) and laying out a plan of action to bolster our confidence, but if we stop at the completion of this intellectual work, never daring to do the emotionally difficult work of trying something new—taking risk—we will not grow.

Practice doesn't necessarily make perfect, but it does make more confident if you pay attention to what you are learning as you try things.

Let's bring this all back to you as a woman of beauty and substance. You started this book hoping perhaps to find some help, encouragement or practical advice. I hope you found what you were looking for. More than that, I hope you have come to believe in a deeper, truer way in your own amazing beauty. You are one of a kind. And you're here for an indeterminate amount of time. It may be a long time; it may be very brief. The number of days counts far less than what you fill them with and how you share what you learn and see and love with people around you.

Many years ago I was practicing with my fifth grade class to sing at an all-school concert. Miss Stevens was directing our practice. She did all the usual conductor stuff—waving her arms and hands in time to the music, nodding at this group then that one to sing or be silent. Her energy was contagious, but what I remember most was the absolute joy that shone from her eyes and spilled from her lips in the most delightful laughter.

When I think of what happiness looks like—and what I want to share with my family and friends—I remember Miss Stevens. I'm sure she had challenges and disappointments in her life. She was a young single woman from Chicago teaching fifth grade in a small town. Did she want to get married? Did she want a family of her own? What did she hope for in her teaching career?

I'll never know. What I do know, however, is at that moment in my young developing mind, I recognized a woman of beauty and substance.

It takes courage to become that kind of woman. The world pushes you and me to be like somebody else if we want to be truly successful. That's bunk. You have what you need to create a life that is happy, meaningful and beautiful. One day and one step at a time you can risk your way to powerful success. I know you can do it. You know it, too. Be strong. Be happy. Be you.

ABOUT THE AUTHOR

Susan A. Marshall is an author, speaker, and Founder of Backbone Institute, LLC, whose mission is to create a stronger, more confident future one person or team at a time. She has been assisting leaders in public and private sector industry, non-profit agencies, and public education for nearly 30 years. Her work is dedicated to building strong leaders who in turn create successful organizations, transform school systems, and develop leaders at all levels.

Susan has had a love of words and writing since childhood. One of six rambunctious kids, she often stole away to the railroad tracks or river to write about the people and events that surrounded her. When John F. Kennedy challenged the nation to "ask what you can do for your country," she was inspired to study and practice leadership. These early seeds took root over a career that has included writing, speaking, and teaching.

Susan's educational career spans nearly two decades and three different universities and features all the starts and stops of a learning life. She persevered over 13 years as a regular student, college dropout, and non-traditional student to earn a bachelor's degree in management. She invested another 2-1/2 years to complete MBA studies.

Her corporate and consulting experience includes work with Fortune 100 companies including GM, Apple, Archer Daniels

Midland and Best Buy as well as a wide variety of private enterprises and non-profits such as New York City Leadership Academy and Boys & Girls Clubs of America. She has been welcomed as a guest-lecturer at several University of Wisconsin campuses and at Marquette University, Alverno College, the University of Michigan Ross School of Business, and the University of Chicago Graduate School of Business.

Her first book, *How to Grow a Backbone: 10 Strategies for Gaining Power and Influence at Work,* has been translated into multiple languages and is especially popular in Asia. Her second book, *Life. Be in it.* was released in December 2012. *Of Beauty and Substance: A Backbone Guide for Women* is the first of six Backbone Guides, each addressing a specific audience. To see the full complement of Guides, visit her website at backboneinstitute.com.

Susan is the mother of two grown daughters and grandmother of five granddaughters. In addition to writing, teaching, and spending time with family, she enjoys reading, exercise, and training her new puppy, Lacy, to become a therapy dog. Susan lives in Oconomowoc, Wisconsin. She welcomes email correspondence at susan@backboneinstitute.com and telephone conversation at 262-567-5983 or 262-689-7763.

Across the US and indeed around the world, an epidemic loss of confidence has eroded all of our most important institutions: families, schools, churches, businesses, non-profit agencies, and governments. In the US, the Conference Board's Consumer Confidence Index of August 2012 shows the lowest level of confidence since late 2011, thanks to a more pessimistic outlook. Failing schools have claimed headlines for too many years, while businesses struggle to find qualified workers and entrepreneurs try to build new companies amid tighter credit terms and growing regulation. Competition for charitable donations threatens non-profits. Changing social mores challenge once-understood norms and political leaders lose trust with every broken promise.

At the foundation of so much disappointment lies a growing sense of personal vulnerability and despair. This is not new in the history of the world, but it is unfamiliar to current generations who have been raised during good times and promised a life of ease. Coping skills, once a staple of everyday learning, were abandoned as growing numbers of people enjoyed what appeared to be endless bounty as a result of gainful employment or government largesse. The result is a sharply reduced ability to deal with life's realities.

Given this erosion of personal and institutional confidence, there is an intense need to rebuild foundations. Backbone Institute offerings answer this need with products and services to instill new competence through mastery of five fundamental skills; elevate confidence through action-based learning; and enable intelligent, purposeful risk to foster sustained growth. *The mission of Backbone Institute is to create a stronger, more confident future one person or team at a time.*

With nearly 30 years of hands-on experience in professional and leadership development, Susan A. Marshall, founder of Backbone Institute, knows that this work is less about providing more information and more about insisting upon practice. Reading leadership books and attending leadership workshops is important as a means of education and inspiration. However, the application of this knowledge in everyday situations is what makes the difference.

Backbone Institute offerings are constructed based on this deep experience and the conviction that action learning—trial and error in some cases—is the best means of truly internalizing learning, applying it to specific situations and gradually changing behavior. Backbone Institute books, bootcamps, podcasts, and keynote addresses deliver a consistent message: In order to elevate confidence and embrace new opportunity, it is necessary to take small systematic steps toward change, compile evidence of success, and broaden experiences in a consistent manner. Backbone Institute offerings combine challenge and accountability with the ongoing support and encouragement so essential to long-term growth.

Organizations that invest in this unique professional development realize top- and bottom-line improvements as employees, managers and leaders convert increased confidence to deeper engagement with their work and organizations. Decisions get made faster and more effectively. Partnerships are strengthened internally and externally. Competent, confident people extend themselves to take intelligent, purposeful risk on behalf of their careers and their organizations.

Individuals who participate in Backbone Bootcamps discover latent capabilities that, when developed, lead to new opportunity and deeper satisfaction.

Testimonials from Backbone Bootcamp participants:

"I'm a big believer in pushing the comfort zone and doing it often. Get out of your safe zone and start learning and growing through experiencing things that scare you...my friend Susan A. Marshall has taught me this and believe it or not, those experiences are what help define us as leaders and those who inspire others to take the same risks. Be the example!"

"I wish I knew some of these things when I was younger. My life skills were so weak, I was afraid of my shadow. This work turned on the light and helped me understand it all!"

"Persevering through some adversity at work was the best confidence booster and lesson I could have had, but I wouldn't have had that perspective without the bootcamp. You have a tremendous amount of insight; you helped me hang on through a rough spell in my life that seemed endless and hopeless."

"This work brings something abstract into something you can actually work with. I wouldn't miss Susan's sessions."

"This really changed how I see myself and has definitely been a boost to my self-esteem."

"This work helped me to face the things that were scary to me and which prevented me from actually believing that I had confidence in who I am now and who I will be in the future."

"The work on assumptions is powerful. It's amazing the things we think we know that simply are not true."

"The Backbone Bootcamp was my lifeline. Today I have a voice, ask for what I need, and let others know when they have crossed a line. I know that others' reactions are not all about me. I have incredible opportunities to be happier, healthier, stronger and far more influential in my work."

CPSIA information can be obtained at www.ICGtesting.com
Printed in the USA
LVOW01s1123060115

421560LV00004B/4/P